HOW TO DO WHAT YOU WANT TO DO

HOW TO DO
WHAT YOU WANT TO DO
The Art of Self-Discipline

by
PAUL A. HAUCK

THE WESTMINSTER PRESS
Philadelphia

Book Design by Dorothy Alden Smith

Published by The Westminster Press®
Philadelphia, Pennsylvania

PRINTED IN THE UNITED STATES OF AMERICA

Library of Congress Cataloging in Publication Data

Hauck, Paul A
  How to do what you want to do.

  1. Self-control. 2. Rational-emotive psychotherapy.
I. Title.
BF632.H28   158'.1   76–15248
ISBN 0–664–24122–0

To my brother, Al, and my sister, Mousie. What would my youth have been without either of you?

CONTENTS

Preface   9

1. Meet a Few Champions
   of Self-Discipline   11

2. Why It's So Easy to Goof Off   18

3. Three Obstacles
   to Self-Discipline   40

4. Techniques of Self-Discipline   59

5. Putting the Techniques to Work   93

6. A Student Struggles
   with Self-Discipline   111

7. Final Remarks   121

PREFACE

WITH THIS BOOK I come to the end of the quartet I conceived four years ago. Although it is the last in the series that I have written on emotional problems, this book should perhaps have been the first because I regard it as the most important of the four. Without self-discipline it is almost impossible to achieve the drive and motivation required to overcome depression, to put in the exertion necessary to conquer hostility, or to dedicate oneself to fighting worries and fears which are constant companions to us all.

I chose to write four books on the subject of emotional disturbances because so frequently the emotional problems I see in my own practice fall under these four headings. Most people coming to psychotherapy will have trouble with one or more of these major disturbances: depression, anger, fear, or poor self-discipline. Therefore I wrote *Overcoming Depression,* in which I pointed out that self-blame, self-pity, and other-pity are three main causes of psychological depression. In *Overcoming Frustration and Anger* I pointed out that the two demands: (1) I must always have my way, and (2)

People are bad and should be severely punished because they do not give me what I want, are the major reasons for psychologically caused hostility. In *Overcoming Worry and Fear* I pointed out that something considered dangerous and fearsome focused upon endlessly was the cause of fear in all its forms, for example, worry, apprehension, nervousness.

Self-discipline is as important a skill to master as is the need to master depression, hostility, or fear. In fact, unless one has mastered self-discipline, the other tasks cannot be mastered at all. If you have the intelligence of a genius but read nothing except comics, you could then be the most gifted person in the whole world but have the achievement level of a mental retardate. You could have the body of a Tarzan, but if you spend your time filling up on beer and pizza, as for being a Tarzan, forget it. Edison said that genius is 10 percent inspiration and 90 percent perspiration. We can be sure that the 90 percent perspiration comes from a great deal of self-discipline.

I therefore make the claim that all of us are a great deal more capable than we ever realize. We seldom achieve our potential, because we are not as disciplined as we need to be to make our talents blossom. If you want to know what you are really capable of, you must learn how to put your nose to the grindstone, work against boredom, learn to take the long easy way in life rather than the short hard way, and make your talents shine as they have never shone before. There is only one way in the world to do that: discipline yourself. This book will attempt to show you how.

Therefore, roll up your sleeves, tighten your belt another notch, take a deep breath. Let's get to work.

1
Meet a Few Champions of Self-Discipline

The Sickly Mountain Climber

During a winter evening several years ago, I listened to a conversation from Los Angeles over the car radio while I was riding home from work. I did not catch the beginning of the interview, but what I heard seemed so amazing that I want to pass the gist of the program on to you.

A man in his sixties was being interviewed who apparently had had a number of psychological and medical problems most of his life. When he was in his thirties he was practically a cripple because of heart and lung trouble. He had developed a number of powerful fears, one of which was a fear of height. He was advised not to strain himself and to be as easy on himself as he possibly could. This he did for years, but his condition did not improve. One day he decided that he was sick and tired of his limited and restricted life and that he would do something about it. That evening he went to a restaurant and while seated at his table glanced up at the wall and saw a picture of Mt. Blanc in France. He decided then and there that he would overcome his fear of height by climbing Mt. Blanc. Shortly thereafter he told his friends about his plans. He told so many of them, in fact, that he could not go back on his promise without being laughed at. Rather than allow that to happen, he began a strenuous training program. He then flew to Europe, hired a guide, and actually climbed Mt. Blanc.

Since then he has scaled it about six times and is aiming for the amateur record of the world by climbing Mt. Blanc one more time. On one occasion he made the ascent in a blizzard while the temperature was thirty degrees below zero. To keep in shape for this grueling task, he jogged several miles every day and swam over a dozen laps in the pool.

It is his contention that Mt. Blanc has saved his life. Instead of being horrified at the prospect of going up the dangerous slopes, he has been drawn to the mountain like a magnet.

Can you imagine the discipline it took for this middle-aged man to develop his body from that of a physical cripple to the point where he could actually keep up with an experienced mountain climber? Can you imagine what it requires to run several miles and swim many laps each day in preparation for such an event? How many excuses would most of us come up with to escape such arduous labor? Yet, despite the enormous expenditure of energy and pain involved in pushing a sickly and aging body to the point of exhaustion, he has saved his life through this very program. In the final analysis, he was able to live in health for a long time simply because he did not evade the heavy responsibility of caring for his body.

Albert Ellis

This gentleman is the founder of the Institute for Advanced Study in Rational Psychotherapy and the school of psychotherapy called Rational-Emotive Therapy (RET). This book is based on the principles put forth by Dr. Ellis. To write a book on self-discipline without including him as one of the finest examples of a self-disciplined person would be an enormous mistake. Anyone who has met him is aware of this characteristic as much as any of his other traits. He is able to work tirelessly, with great efficiency, and does it practically single-handedly.

In his everyday life this clinical psychologist gets to work at about nine in the morning and works straight through until eleven at night, with a short break for lunch·and one for supper. He then reviews his mail, dictates or types his correspondence, and does reading as time allows. On Saturday nights he quits work about suppertime and often busies himself with matters of the Institute or writes books. On many weekends he is off flying around the country giving speeches or leading group marathons. He has published over two hundred articles in professional journals and has written over thirty books on psychotherapy, marriage counseling, and sex. By himself he is able to turn out a quantity of work that would equal the output of a small mental health center. Although I have no figures to prove this, I would not be at all surprised if it were eventually demonstrated that Albert Ellis has the largest psychotherapeutic practice in the whole world.

The beauty of it is that he is able to accomplish all this

with ease, with an absence of painful stress, and with a joy for his work. The belief that work *has* to make you upset or exhausted simply does not apply when we see how he disciplines himself.

Winfield Overton Franklin

Another example of a champion of self-discipline is a seventy-five-year-old man who has conditioned his body in the most extraordinary way imaginable. Although most people seventy-five years old are retiring, walking around with bent shoulders, ready to kick the bucket, this man takes over one hundred vitamins a day and has not had a cold in fifty-eight years. He gets up at dawn every day, and runs fifty miles a week. He once did five thousand sit-ups without resting.

How did he get in this incredible shape? *He pushes himself* a little bit beyond his limit whenever he wants to improve. This means that he is never terribly uncomfortable with his tasks, since he increases them so gradually as to be almost imperceptible.

Perhaps the most unusual thing he did was to run *seventy-five miles on his seventy-fifth birthday.* This whole story was covered in the Parade Magazine section of the *Times Democrat* in Davenport, Iowa, on May 20, 1973. It shows this robust seventy-five-year-old man running around the track while his wife is counting the laps. And wouldn't you know, he added one more lap for good measure! Even on his birthday he pushed himself.

If you need an example of what fantastic things self-discipline can accomplish, it seems to me this gentleman and his accomplishments have got to be an inspiration.

14

The San Francisco Waiter

One night I was watching television's *Johnny Carson Show* and saw an interview with a man 106 years old. The remarkable thing about him was that he has been running to work every morning for years, a distance of six miles. At this same age he entered a race and ran seven miles in less than one hour, and he has an official paper to prove it. Try doing that sometime when you are a hundred years old.

Recently I tested my cardiorespiratory index and wanted to see how fast I could run a mile and a half. I did it in twelve minutes and forty-seven seconds and I was almost completely bushed even though I had jogged almost daily for at least six months.

Isaac Asimov

There is only one way in the world that Mr. Asimov could have written over one hundred books in his life so far: great self-discipline. He sometimes writes several in one year. And these are not simple or brief books. Some of them are very weighty and scholarly works.

When we realize that some people take all day to write a letter, it is obvious that he is so well self-disciplined and trained at this point in his life that he is able to write whole chapters in a day. Some people sweat and strain to write one book in their lifetime, while this fellow goes on season after season writing three or four a year. How is this possible? He knows what he wants, he knows that hard work will get it for him, and so he decides to face the problem rather than avoid it. And that is one of the secrets of self-discipline.

Michelangelo

It took Michelangelo four and a half years to paint the Sistine Chapel ceiling. He lay on his back day after day painting on wet plaster, creating a masterpiece, despite the fact that he did not particularly enjoy painting. Sculpturing was his real love. Again, relentless self-discipline had to be called upon to achieve some of the masterpieces of art that we know him by today. His statue of *David* and his *Pietà* are only two fascinating and fantastic examples of artistic talent and of self-discipline as well. To chip away at a rock is in itself a terribly laborious and time-consuming pursuit. No matter what his talent, unless he had the stamina and the self-discipline to use that talent, his monumental pieces of work would never have seen the light of day.

Miscellaneous Examples

Can you imagine a blind man playing par golf? It's possible and has been done. A fellow in California ran twenty-five marathons in a year (which is remarkable enough). But when you realize that he had no toes, heels, or balls of his feet, you can begin to appreciate how great his self-discipline must have been to develop such stamina and endurance.

How about the man who holds the national football record for kicking the longest field goal? He has no toes.

An Olympic swimmer won two gold and two silver medals two days after he had an operation for a collapsed lung. What does it take to perform a feat like that? Undoubtedly a lot of courage and self-confidence.

But where do they come from? Usually from enormous self-discipline.

Rev. Bob Richards, a former Olympic champion, reassures us that one does not have to be a giant to be a champion. One does have to be self-disciplined, however. This explains why 95 percent of the champions in the world are 5 feet 10 inches and under and weigh 175 pounds or less. Weaklings of the world, take heart! All is not lost. Make up in self-discipline what you lack in muscle and you could become a superman in physical or nonphysical pursuits. Ever hear of Gandhi?

These are some of the champions among many who have shown us the way to self-discipline. We may not agree with their goals but we can certainly applaud the control they had over themselves to achieve those goals. They were masters of their own destiny because they knew the secret to self-discipline. Without it, all their talents and best intentions would have been no different from the annual resolutions all of us make and seldom follow through on. That is exactly why most of us are not champions.

What I want is to help you to have self-discipline at *your* command. Then you can use it when you want to, not when somebody says you must or when you're down-and-out and all other options are gone. Life can be so much easier if you have this talent available at your beck and call. You have the potential for self-discipline—we all do. What we need is control over when to use it or not use it. This will be one of the major purposes of this book: to help you *to do what you really want to do when you want to do it.*

2
Why It's So Easy to Goof Off

BEFORE WE DELVE into the techniques of developing good self-discipline, let us ask why self-discipline is such a difficult skill to develop. Why do we have such repeated problems with it?

Poor Self-Discipline Is a Natural Trait

Certain behaviors are by nature easy for us and other behaviors are difficult. Avoiding a difficult situation seems like the most natural course to take because we are so easily seduced by immediate satisfaction. That is the way we humans are made.

Man does not enjoy frustrations. Therefore he wants to remove them immediately and take the quickest road to relief. However, that does not mean that to do so is sensible or healthy. As I shall try to show in the following pages, getting to your pleasure the quickest way possible may be pleasant for the moment but in the long run it can be terribly expensive and painful.

An Infant Has to Have His Way to Survive

The whole focus of an infant is short-range pleasure. If a child has to wait too long for his feeding, he can become seriously ill. He must have enough sleep or he will be irritable. He must not remain soiled too long lest his tender skin develop a rash or an infection. In other words, we have all been conditioned to having our needs gratified rather rapidly. This is the reason we survived those fragile childhood years. But this conditioning has cost us something. It was healthy and of value at one time in our lives. But we must now break this expectation of getting everything we want quickly and realize that, as adults, this is no longer the case. In fact, the opposite is often true: getting what we want quickly is often the harmful method of satisfying ourselves. Taking things the slow way is easier and less painful.

Poor Self-Discipline Seems to Pay Off

Insurance companies are perfectly aware of the greed some people show in faking illnesses in order to get big settlements in the courts. Instead of living life to its fullest and developing their talents, some people are content to let an accident get them down because the rewards for not being able to work the rest of their lives are financially attractive. These people are merely settling for the immediate, not the long-range benefits. Rather than learn a new skill and make it back on the job, a mechanic might prefer to get a $50,000 settlement and then spend the next several years rocking back and forth on his porch doing absolutely nothing.

The tendency on the part of society to reward poor self-discipline is becoming an increasingly serious problem. People are using emotional disturbances in particular as a way of avoiding stressful situations. They have nervous breakdowns to get out of frustrating jobs, to get their way with their mates, or to command sympathy and attention. Instead of working at problems the hard way by eventually mastering them and becoming adults in the process, they resort to a dramatic and hysterical kind of collapse. It gets them results, to be sure, but it costs dearly in the long run. Such persons never grow up to be the people they might have been. To continue getting their way, they must have emotional scenes repeatedly. They shake nervously, pull their hair, throw dishes, worry over having a heart attack, and show other signs of nervous distress. Unfortunately, industry is making it easy for people to be hospitalized for emotional problems, and you can bet your bottom dollar that the undisciplined person, whenever he wants a vacation from this tough old world, is either going to get depressed and nervous, drink too much, or attempt suicide. He'll be hospitalized in a modern hospital, be given lots of attention and sympathy, and he won't have to go to work for as long as he can show enough disturbance to justify being there. In short, the insurance company and the company he works for (which wants him back on the job as soon as possible) are rewarding him for being sick and encouraging him to stay away.

Adults whose injuries cannot be completely disproved will be sorely tempted to become the worst kind of malingerers imaginable. They will then decide to live in the lap of luxury and refuse to recover from their various ailments simply because they are receiving comfortable financial payments for having them. This very reward which they receive for the injury makes it hard for them to want to develop the stamina and discipline it takes to overcome their handicaps.

Suppose a soldier has a 75 percent disability because of an injury to his legs. This may seem like a generous gesture on the part of an appreciative country for the service this young man rendered. However, unless he has character, he is likely to feel overly secure in these monthly payments and will not work to overcome his handicap to the point where he does not need that monthly check. The payment then becomes a means for him to remain crippled and never apply himself as much as he otherwise might.

Industry is repeatedly facing this problem with persons who have injured their backs or who have suffered emotional problems. The moment this happens these people are sometimes laid off from work with comfortable benefits. It is extremely tempting not to get better when you are being paid to be sick. Therefore those who receive such benefits sometimes go for interminable periods of time living typically indulged and poorly self-disciplined lives simply because they are momentarily comfortable. It would be so much better for them in the long run if they did not depend upon that money, if they learned how to resist being an emotional cripple and tried to get off the benefits as quickly as possible.

I have seen instance after instance of people going into psychiatric units of hospitals with all expenses paid. I have observed how they were not motivated as they might have been if they had not had such generous company benefits. To be somewhat anxious about their situations would have made them a great deal healthier because it would have made them work that much harder on their anxieties or their depressions. When one knows that the wolf is at the door one cannot afford to complain about hangnails, headaches, or blue moods. This is sometimes what insurance coverage by industry or government tends to do to us. We become lax and soft and take advantage of what was meant to be an enormous help and a charitable act during times of great crisis and need. And one of the saddest fallouts from this whole process is that some people with good work histories who have had ambition all their lives now become emotional cripples. They rely on the secondary gain that they derive from the payments they receive. This is a regrettable waste of human talent, and it happens all too frequently. In the final analysis it comes to nothing but poor self-discipline. They think it is easier to avoid a difficult task, such as to recover from an illness, than it is to face all the hard work required to get on their feet again.

Gambling is a particularly enticing habit that sometimes pays off quickly and handsomely. The man who is impatient to become rich can easily be lured to the racetrack or the gaming table, where a lucky break might make him rich. Despite the fact that the odds are against him, he comes back repeatedly to these pie-in-the-sky solutions to achieve what is usually accomplished only through hard work and talent. The fact that one can make an occasional killing at the risk of only a couple of dollars seems to spur on these impatient persons to think they shouldn't have to work at all. So they wind up gambling away all their money.

Tim was such a person. It absolutely infuriated him to see others so much better off than he. He had tried the technique of working hard and saving his money and he actually accumulated a fairly good-sized bank account. But this *long easy way* was simply too slow for him. He decided to go at things the *short hard way.* He therefore began to play poker nightly and to visit the local racetrack. In no time at all he lost all that he had saved. During that period he had a couple of winners, to be sure, but it was never enough to compensate for his great losses.

His downfall was his mistaken belief that the short way was the easy way.

One person whom I counseled was sent to me by the courts. He had been caught shoplifting expensive clothing from one of the finer stores in town. He confessed that he had been quite successful for the past several years at shoplifting merchandise valued at tens of thousands of dollars from the local merchants.

He was a clotheshorse and needed to dress himself up like a peacock wherever he went. He obviously did not have the funds for this, so he simply stole what he needed. To justify this outright theft he used the most blatant and infantile kinds of rationalizations. For example, he insisted that it didn't matter that he stole from the stores, because they were all insured. Besides, he was poor, they were rich. I tried hard to get him to realize that he had no business stealing other people's money no matter how much they had. I told him that by his stealing he was increasing the cost of the merchandise to other potential buyers. He still went on believing it was right to do what he was doing. He had a strong inferiority complex that melted away wonderfully the moment he put on a beautiful garment. He also thought it was easier to steal than to work. For instance, I pointed out to him that he was now talking to a psychologist, he had a record, and the courts were about ready to throw him in jail for several years because of his activities. How could he still insist that he had been doing things the easy way? He took the short way, to be sure, but certainly it was the hard way in the long run.

The difficult part of the treatment came in trying to get him to stop shoplifting since he had always been so successful in the past. He knew he had a 5-to-1 chance of succeeding, and as long as the odds were that good he was willing to take them. I told him quite honestly that I thought he might not stop his habit until he was actually sent to jail for a period of time. He agreed that this might be exactly what it would take to convince him that he was behaving unwisely. In this case a prison term rather than psychotherapy would have made more sense, because we were dealing with a person who had little sense of ethical values as far as other people's property was concerned. He was also a person who was essentially immature and spoiled. Although he complained all the time about how deprived he had been as a child, he was still a spoiled individual as an adult. He believed quite honestly that the world owed him a living and that he had the right to filch other people's property from them simply because they had not had to go through his kind of deprived upbringing. Such people often do not learn through moralizing lectures. They usually have to be taught through hard experience that whether they agree with us or not, they are going to wind up hurting themselves in the long run. Ultimately experience is the great teacher which helps the un-self-disciplined person to realize that what he is doing for himself is really not all that good.

As I suspected, Bill, the successful shoplifter, could not keep his hands off other people's goods. He was arrested again and this time was sent to prison.

Many people in the mental health field would have explained his behavior by pointing to his being depressed, his attempting to overcome inferiority feelings by wearing fancy duds, or his having a deep-seated hostility against a society that deprived him as a child. All of these may be true in part. But the aspect that most professionals would miss in this case is that we are dealing purely and simply with a person who has not learned to discipline himself. More often than most psychotherapists realize, people are in trouble because they simply have not grown up and learned to live with frustrations. Bill would have been a perfectly capable man with no serious emotional hangups if he had simply learned how to tolerate frustration, to lump it if he couldn't change the problem, and to work hard toward his goals rather than think he had to have immediate relief for his current frustrations. If he had purchased his clothes rather than stolen them, he would have been better off all the way around.

Escapism Gives Quick Results

One of the most attractive things about poor self-discipline is the fact that it is immediately rewarding. How can you fight something that gives you immediate relief from a stressful situation? If you are afraid of crowds and have a couple of drinks before you go to a party to make you feel confident, it's easy to see how you're going to resort to that quick solution in the future.

When you are home alone and wishing you could have a large circle of friends but you are afraid of being rejected, just think how pleasant it might be to fantasize yourself as a great person, world famous, with everyone knocking at your door. The satisfaction that you could get without any real effort would be enormous and sure to be repeated because it would be so delightful and so easy.

When you are confronted with a bully and you escape by running away, you are bound to experience immediate relief. But you haven't learned how to defend yourself and you may be in the same danger again tomorrow.

All these experiences give us the firm conviction that the avoidance of a difficult situation is immediately gratifying and is to be preferred over anything that keeps us in an unpleasant situation. This is why the drug culture has grown so enormously. Our youth and others have resorted to drugs not only because their friends apply social pressures but also because escape with drugs is so complete and swift. The young man who was not able to get a job today can make everything right with the world if he simply shoots something in his arm that night. The young girl who is not very popular and who has never made the effort to develop into an interesting person needs only to swallow a bunch of junk and she feels like the Queen of the May. The temptation in these and many other situations like them is enormous and often cannot compete against fighting the temptation.

Refusing to Accept Reality

Before you can discipline yourself to overcome an unpleasant state of affairs, you will first have to accept the fact that reality must be faced. To go on a diet, to get up early to go to work, to speak in front of a large group of people are specific examples. It does you no good whatever to insist pigheadedly that you should not have to get up early in the morning, that you should have been given the gift of gab so that you would not be nervous before an auditorium full of people, and that nature made a big mistake when it made people with a tendency to get fat.

All these statements make no sense whatever, because there is no reason why the world *should* be any different from what it is. You are simply behaving like a child if you go around stating that because you don't like the world, it has to be different. This infantile grandiosity is most ridiculous. Ultimately it is bound to be an enormous deterrent toward disciplining yourself to face these very annoyances. If you keep telling yourself all day long that the frustrations should not exist, how are you to discipline yourself against them? You must first recognize a problem before you can work against it. By insisting that things should not be a certain way, you are not recognizing that they *are* that way. If it means that you have to go hungry in order to lose weight and you don't like that idea, then learn to lump it. Just don't go around complaining that losing weight involves being uncomfortable. Of course it does, and that's too bad. But that's the way it is.

And don't complain about how unfair it is that you have to do this while others may not. If you have the kind of physical constitution that turns everything into fat, but your friend eats three times as much and still looks like a starving bird, don't moan and groan to the heavens about what a rotten world it is. Of course this is often a rotten and unfair world. As one of my clients said, "This is a stinking world, and you have to get used to the smell." And I guarantee that if you learn to accept what you can't change, the fact that man gets hungry when he does not eat or that social systems require him to work more than he sleeps, you will eventually become a more mature person.

Boredom

Joe was one of those gifted people who could do any number of things if he stuck to it. He was a good athlete. He could get a job practically any time he wanted to. He was a witty and charming fellow who sometimes treated his friends badly, but had such a winning style that he was always forgiven and still had a great many friends. But the guy was almost a complete flop in nearly anything he attempted. It was a miracle that he got through high school. That was probably the last time he had a real feeling of success. The major reason for his lack of achievement was that he was such a pleasure-loving fool. Any time he attempted anything and got to the point where things stopped being fun, he simply got bored and quit.

What Joe didn't seem to realize was that boredom is part and parcel to any endeavor that is undertaken. Whether it be listening to great music, eating wonderful food, making love, skiing, or whatever, it is impossible to do anything that one ordinarily enjoys without sometimes becoming bored. Woe to the man who cannot tolerate some boredom, for he shall forever be bored.

That's the pity of it all. The person who cannot tolerate boredom never plows through the muck of hard work which is necessary to reach the higher and more interesting levels of achievement. Instead, when he gets stuck in boredom he turns around and tries another approach to the mountaintop—and runs into another swamp. He goes back and forth around the base of the mountain trying to cross the swamps and never gets to where he wants to go. The trouble with people who stop at the boredom phase is that they think boredom is *terrible*.

Take the case of a typical high school student. He does not do his history, because he is bored. He literally thinks that because he is bored he is justified in not working. I have talked to such young people numerous times and conversations like the following ensue:

CLIENT: If only I weren't bored, I would be able to get through that class, but I can't go home and study at night if I don't like it.

THERAPIST: Who says you can't? Why can't you work hard even though you're bored? Can't you work very hard at something and be bored at the same time?

C: Of course not. Anybody knows that you can't do your best if you have no interest in something.

T: I didn't say you would do your best. All I am saying is that you *can* do the job even though you don't like it and even though it bores the living daylights out of you. If you wait until you are excited about something before you do it, I guarantee that you will not achieve very much in life. Your problem is that you think it is horrible to be bored, and that boredom has to stop everything you are doing. Why does it? You can put *some* time in on your task even though you don't like it and even though it bores you for the time being. However, the more effort you put into it, the more skill you will gain and the more you may then enjoy the activity. Therefore, to overcome your boredom, let me recommend that you work *twice* as hard during those periods of boredom so that you will create a renewed interest in your task and thereby kill the boredom itself.

This typical student couldn't see what I was driving at right away. Over a period of several weeks he began to think more rationally about his habit and began to try my suggestions. Instead of excusing himself because he was bored with school, he decided to go home and apply himself. He found that the more effort he put into studying, the more he enjoyed it. This began to raise his grades, which gave him a new incentive to study more. As he did so, he began to discover a great many things that interested him. His boredom soon disappeared. And, incidentally, he also avoided the danger of having to repeat a grade—the last thing in the world that he wanted to do. This achievement, however, would not have been possible if he had continued to consider occasional boredom to be a catastrophe.

When you find yourself in a similar situation, first of all anticipate boredom and remember *(a)* that it is bound to happen sometimes, and *(b)* that it is not all *that* bad. If you will stay with the task and work *harder* during the bored phase, you will soon come out the other side with a new interest, ready to discover wonderful and fascinating things about the task you are undertaking.

Spite, Fear, and Rationalization

These three neurotic conditions often account for the reasons why people cannot discipline themselves well. They are fairly easily understood, so I shall not go into them at great length in each case, but will just give a brief illustration. The last condition, rationalization, is a bit more interesting and is often at such an unconscious level that it deserves a closer examination. I shall present part of a verbatim transcript from a counseling session with a young girl which illustrates that problem admirably.

SPITE

If you were constantly pestered by your parents and you felt they were trying to run your life, it would be simple to resist them. If their orders to you were to lose weight, study hard, clean out the garage, and so on, you might find yourself vengefully and spitefully doing just the opposite merely to prove that they really cannot make you do their bidding. It is not as though you do not have the self-discipline to accomplish those feats. Rather, you are angry at being ordered to do them and it makes you refuse to apply good self-discipline to get the job done. We refer to this condition as a power struggle. Each individual is trying to prove to the other just who is in control.

If your husband orders you to clean up the house, you may find yourself becoming so angry and hurt at this inconsiderateness that you deliberately and spitefully make the house dirtier. That's both getting revenge and proving at the same time that he really cannot make you clean up the house if you don't want to. Even though you may have wanted to clean the house, you are now going against your own wishes.

That's not so bad in the matter of the house. But suppose you refused to lose weight just to spite your mate? Unfortunately this often happens and makes good self-discipline impossible. It isn't that you couldn't discipline yourself, it is only that you are fully intent on proving that you are more powerful. You simply refuse to apply your good self-discipline to the task.

Rather than get involved in power struggles, allow the other person the right to dictate to you. If your mate tells you to stop smoking and you really want to, don't say spitefully that he or she can't make you stop smoking. That's self-evident. Nobody can make you lose weight, clean up your house, or stop smoking unless you want to. So stop proving a point that is obvious. It isn't necessary. Simply determine for yourself whether or not this is really what you want to do. If you really want to run your own life, then don't let someone else's demands turn you away from what you want. If you want to stop smoking and you do the opposite because you were ordered to stop, then obviously you aren't in control of yourself at all. You are reacting to what someone else said. In effect, your spouse's words are controlling you even though it happens to be in the totally opposite direction from what you wanted. You are not running your life, it is your spouse, or your boss, or whoever.

Just think what a pushover you are for other people when it is realized that you behave out of a sense of revenge or you engage in the power struggle game. If, for example, a man is irritated at his wife's slowness in getting to the supper dishes, all he has to do is tell her he hates people who jump up after supper and insist that she sit and talk over coffee. Then he is likely to get her to do the dishes promptly.

Therefore, be your own boss. Don't get involved with power struggles. Each of us is master of ourselves to the point where nobody can make us do a great many things unless it is by brute force.

FEAR

Fear is the second of this trio which neurotically interferes with self-discipline. Fear of failure, fear of being criticized, or the fear of something else can block doing what you want to do. For example, I once worked with a fellow for some months on his self-discipline toward losing weight and got absolutely nowhere. It appeared to me that he had to have another psychological reason for maintaining his three hundred pounds but he absolutely refused to admit that there was anything he was afraid of. I suggested that he might be afraid of the kind of social life he would be expected to lead if he lost weight. Or that he would be expected to work harder, and so on. He denied all this, so we simply went back to working on the self-discipline problem itself. Each week he would lose a little bit and shortly thereafter regain it. After this went on for some weeks, it became apparent to him that he had to be putting on the weight for some reason he didn't understand. It was only then that he was willing to explore what it might be and to stop resisting my interpretations concerning any other factors that were encouraging him to eat rather than to diet.

As he went deeper into his background it was realized that he had many socially rejecting experiences. He feared that if he lost weight, he would be expected to socialize and thus would risk rejection. As long as he had his weight he knew that no girl would go out with him and that his social life would be extremely limited. That in itself was comforting and it protected him against rejection. When he began to understand that he

33

was actually afraid of socializing, he began to pay attention to his diet. He reminded himself that even though he faced the possibility of rejection, that was not as bad as carrying around three hundred pounds. Once he knew *why* he was refusing to diet he was able to control the dieting much better. Eventually he got to the point where his self-image improved considerably and he was less afraid of rejection.

RATIONALIZATION

People with poor self-discipline are somewhat like alcoholics. They give themselves the fanciest excuses you can imagine for believing whatever they want to believe. One of the clearest examples of rationalization comes from a girl who was doing badly in school although she had the ability to earn decent grades. She was also doing a considerable amount of shoplifting for what she considered to be good reasons. She did not discipline herself to stop this stealing, because she actually talked herself into thinking it was okay. The following is a portion of one of the sessions I recorded when I heard these startling comments.

CLIENT: I haven't stolen anything for a long, long time.
THERAPIST: Why not?
C: Well, I just don't need it.
T: You mean you might have stolen something if you needed it?
C: Well, I can, you know, anytime, if I want to.
T: Have you been tempted to steal? Have you seen a few things around that you—
C: Instead of stealing money, I'll get some candy or

something like that. Nothing big.

T: You mean you did steal bigger things but now you are stealing little things?

C: It isn't necessary. And I don't steal wastefully either. I tell my friends there are two kinds of vandalism: constructive and destructive. Destructive is when you throw bottles out in the street and flatten people's tires. You don't know who you could hurt. Could be your mom coming down the street. Plus your deposit on the bottle.

If you are going to be constructive about stealing, then someone is going to benefit from it. If you are taking from someone else, you gain something right there. And if you sell it to someone else for a low price, you're going to get a little bit of money and make somebody else happy. But if I steal something—I stole something about two weeks ago and I found out I didn't want it. It was a twenty-dollar item and I could have sold it for a dollar or thrown it away. I took it back to the store and put it right where I got it. I just don't believe in this destructive stuff. I only steal for a worthy cause. These kids that steal and break windows and do that kind of stuff, I never did get into that and never will, I don't think.

T: Sometimes it's very tempting to steal and have a few extra pennies. But do you consider the fact that, although it may be very nice for the moment, if you get caught—even with a candy bar—you can build up a record for yourself and perhaps spend time in jail over a piece of candy? Do you stop to think then that it is easier to face a difficult situation—such as going hungry and waiting until you get home to have a candy bar—than it is to steal?

C: Right. There is no hurry, because it is so easy to

steal food, this sweet stuff. But if I don't want sweet stuff, because it gives me acne, then I'll take an apple. I'll go over and pick it up and eat it.

T: But that's not the point, you see. It really is easier at that moment to deny yourself the apple, because if you don't, you will pay for it later and very dearly.

C: How?

T: Well, you may get caught. In the long run you are better off not risking it. In the long run you are better off *facing* a difficult situation than avoiding it. Remember I said that before? That is partly why you have gotten into trouble and why, unless you watch it, you are going to get into more trouble. You're going to hurt yourself more and more. That's up to you. Nobody can stop you. I know I can't. It's not up to me to do so. It's up to you. You can walk out of here and say, "Wow, this guy is nuts," which you may have thought already. But I guarantee you that if you keep up what you've been doing, I'm sure you're going to wind up in trouble. There is no question about it, because you're running your life the hard way. You're getting little bits of pleasure here and there, but in the long run you're hurting yourself very badly.

C: I didn't get caught.

T: But you're going to. It is not a question of *if.* You may get away with it this time or the next time, but you're going to get caught if you keep it up. Every time you get away with it you get more courage to take more. Eventually you are going to run out of luck just as surely as jails have iron bars. The chances of your getting away with stealing a hundred times out of a hundred are ridiculous. I know you may not believe that, and you may have to learn the hard way first. I warned your mother about this today too. We can tell you, but whether you will take the advice or not is really up to you. I told her, "Let her get hurt until she sees for herself." For example, you got drunk the other night. Correct?

C: Yes.

T: I'm sure your mother has told you before that you have to watch how much you drink. Right?

C: Yes.

T: You didn't believe it, so you got drunk. Now you know. See? Okay, that was luckily a harmless experience. You were miserable the next day, and that's the end of that.

C: Yes.

T: But some of these mistakes you make are not going to be forgotten that easily. You don't just suffer for it one day. Some of these mistakes could make you suffer for years.

How about schooling? If you don't get yourself proper schooling so that you can get a degree and get into the kind of profession or trade you want, it's something you may have to live with for the rest of your life. That's the point.

C: If I could sell drugs, I could make a living doing that. It's so easy.

T: For a time perhaps, but your luck has got to run out.

C: Well, if you're going to make a career of selling drugs, yes. But this temporary stuff is—

T: But the point is that it is not becoming temporary with you. When you get tempted and you see something you really like, you still give into temptation and steal. One of these days, because you'll yield to temptation once too often. Sooner or later you *have* to slip.

C: Not necessarily. After you get caught or after you

have done it for a while you know which places are watched and which aren't. I know some kids who know all the angles of shoplifting. They know where the cameras are or if there are mirrors or clerks who are undercover people. Like down at Eastpark. I know just about everybody down there and every store that has cameras. I don't shoplift there anymore but I used to.

T: How do you feel about that? Don't you think there is something immoral and unethical about this? You wouldn't want people stealing from you, would you?

C: No.

T: Well, why do you do to others what you don't want them to do to you?

C: Well, that's a pretty good question. Moral standards these days are getting so low. Let's face the facts. Society today is accepting more and more things by bits and pieces.

T: Well, shoplifting is still illegal. Stealing is stealing. And you're trying to make it into nothing. You are saying, "Well, it's not so bad." But if somebody took anything of yours, you'd squawk, wouldn't you?

C: Yes.

T: Why? Aren't you the one convincing yourself that it's all right to steal, you know—constructive stealing and destructive stealing?

C: Well, it is, you know.

T: I disagree. You've taken a wrong principle and you're trying to justify stealing by saying, "Well, I got some money out of it and somebody got a nice coat." You had no business stealing the coat in the first place. You talk yourself into fairyland stuff. Don't give yourself a cock-and-bull story about how it is all right or how society tolerates more. We just have more people like you around who think it's all right. That's the difference. Don't you see that?

C: Yes. It could be.

T: I wish parents were firmer on this. I wish that when you were taken to court, they had let you sit in jail for a couple of weeks. They didn't do that, did they?

C: No. They just talk to you a little bit.

T: They give you a little sermon and then send you home. Did it bother you at all?

C: Well, I wasn't sad about it, you know. I was only concerned about my odds for getting caught.

T: I see. And you are aware that I have told your parents that should you get caught again, they are not to help you?

C: Not to help me?

T: Yes, they are not to help you. If they help you, what is that going to do with that habit of yours?

C: I don't know. It would make me think Mom would come and help out.

T: That's right. You won't tend to stop, you will tend to increase your shoplifting, because you will say, "Well, I've always gotten my folks to bail me out." I don't want that to happen to you. I want to see you get control over this habit. I don't want to see them unwittingly help you become a crook, which is what you are apparently rapidly becoming. And one of the ways by which that might be avoided is to let you suffer for your mistakes. That is something they haven't let you do. And I hope that they let you suffer with your mistakes so that you will have better sense next time.

C: That's the way it should be.

T: Yes. I'm glad you see that.

39

3
Three Obstacles
to Self-Discipline

Parental Spoiling

Youngsters who are babied and catered to all their lives will virtually have to grow up with a serious problem of self-discipline. They may have intelligence, charm, exposure, and education—most of the ingredients for success. Yet because they have been spoiled all their lives, they have seldom known what it means not to get their way. They have not learned to achieve success through real hard work, to tolerate frustration, to plug away at a task after repeatedly failing. They simply do not know how to apply themselves strenuously for a time without having fun or pleasure.

People raised with indulgence are to be pitied. They can only be helped when gradually thrown on their own resources. Whatever we do we must not baby them any more than their loving but mistaken parents have already done.

Ted comes from a successful professional business family. Both parents are college graduates who provided this bright teen-ager with all the tools and opportunities for growth except one. As a result of spoiling him badly he is an insecure goof-off, delightful when he gets his own way but a neurotic of the first order when frustrated. Small wonder, when we learn how he was raised.

His folks, although capable and bright in every other area of their lives—giving orders at the office, asserting themselves with their peers—were positive jellyfish when asserting themselves against this boy. If he was told to clean up his room and he let it slide, his mother did it. If he didn't take out the garbage, his executive father did. But these are only openers.

If Junior expected a bad day at school and wanted to sleep late, his dad would cheerfully write him an excuse. Ted put it this way: "If they were going to let me get out of taking a test, I figured I was a fool not to take advantage of the chance."

But wait, there's more. When Ted had a paper or a book report to do, he'd go to his bright folks, tell them how pressed he was, and wouldn't they please read the book and write the report for him. And they did! Often he was able to cajole his folks into doing his daily homework for days on end. Luckily he was bright enough to earn average grades, and this is what pulled him through most of high school.

The gradual but steady realization that he was becoming less capable of dealing with life soon led him to escape through drugs and finally to become a social dropout. Now, after going that route for several years and getting nowhere, he is receiving counseling to develop good self-discipline. His task is made immeasurably more difficult by the fact that neither parent is tough enough with him yet, so he must deal with this problem by himself. Never having learned how to deny himself anything, he often feels lost when he tries to

41

conquer his self-indulgence. His folks are ready at his beck and call to indulge him the moment he wants it. Needless to say he is frequently tempted to chuck the self-discipline routine and allow them to baby him again.

Ruth is one of those mothers who did the same thing for her son, Bill. This boy lied and manipulated people ever since he was in second grade. Assurance from the grandfather that the youngster would outgrow the habit lulled Ruth into a sense of complacency. Thereafter, when he acted irresponsibly she avoided punishing him but instead let the boy's fresh and impertinent demands dictate to her.

As he grew older he had no inner resources to deny himself anything. Rather than save his money and then purchase his goodies, he bought whatever he desired and ran up bills so big that only his parents could bail him out. If they protested, he would act hurt, angry, accuse them of not loving him. Sometimes he would even threaten suicide. This was the clincher which always worked.

Eventually it got so bad that the young man would have to leave town every once in a while until he could discourage the bill collectors. But even when he worked in a distant city he would occasionally call home for funds in such a desperate state that his retired folks would send him up to $1,000 at a time to keep him out of jail. By the time they came for counseling they had dipped heavily into their savings and had even sold their farm.

Emphatically I pointed out to them that they had spoiled him badly and unless they let him suffer the consequences of his actions, he was never likely to act more wisely. Even if he threatened suicide, I advised them to refuse to help. Their little baby was now a man in his thirties and if they didn't make him face his responsibilities now, he'd bleed them of every cent they had.

Such talk is hard to give to decent and loving people, but the reality of the situation had to be faced. They left my office with a firm resolve to refuse him help again. The opportunity arrived sooner than we expected.

A few days after my session with them he phoned his parents to inform them he was penniless and that they had to telegraph him funds. Gritting her teeth, his mother told him to get a job, go to the welfare office, the Salvation Army, beg or borrow to get through the next few days and then to watch his spending more carefully. He hung up in disgust. That evening she couldn't eat and that night she couldn't sleep. It was tempting to call and assure him of her continued support. My repeated statements, however, that their overindulgence through the years had turned out to be an unhealthy and unloving act, helped her resist making the call. I supported her move the next morning when she phoned for reassurance.

Needless to say, this first step was followed by others, all geared to unspoil this man, make him strong, disciplined, and independent.

Sometimes it is not the parents who continue to spoil youngsters. It is our schools and other institutions. Adam is one of those bright and charming kids who can make mud turn into whipped cream. As a result he goes through life conning people into making one exception for him after another, in spite of his parents' opposition. They know what a gift of gab he has and that people give in to him against his own best interest. Even though they lowered the boom on him a long time ago, he still manages to be a short-range pleasure seeker outside the home.

For instance, several times he was overdrawn on his bank account, and each time the bank made light of it. The parents asked that he be given a fine, that charges be placed against him, or that at the very least his account be closed. Nothing of the sort happened.

Even more frustrating to the parents was the school's refusal to be firm when Adam clearly deserved to fail. His psychopathic charm and string of excuses always got him out of a jam. Sensing that Adam was gradually being trained by the bank and the school to be a first-class self-indulger, they asked that he be treated fairly and be flunked. The school refused.

When Adam came to see me I found it impossible to convince Mr. Smoothie that he was heading for trouble. Where was my proof that his conduct would backfire someday? The benefits from poor self-discipline were evident, and he knew it. Time, of course, was on my side and on the parents' side. The day will come when he will be expected to have cash to back up his purchases. The day will come when he'll want to attend a school. *Then* he'll pay for his lassitude.

Perfectionism

A great many people who have poor self-discipline are aware of their problem, but are in fact quite comfortable with it. They goof off regularly and love every minute of it even though knowing that someday they are going to pay dearly for it. All of us know people who are smoking themselves to death and they stand a good chance of getting emphysema or lung cancer and yet they would not think of cutting down their smoking one little bit.

However, there are other people who are trying desperately to be more self-disciplined but for neurotic and unconscious reasons are unable to accomplish this. Listen to what one of my students in my psychology class wrote concerning her personality weaknesses.

"I suppose my worst neurosis is the fear of not succeeding. This feeling definitely does me more harm than good. Rather than driving me on to achieve goals, it hinders me to the point of procrastination. I am afraid to even attempt to start on a plan, particularly a long-range plan. If on the way I get discouraged, it will set me back and cause me to waste time, and thus intensify this fear. I can come to the point where I will do absolutely nothing: not go to work, not go to school. Freud said that laziness is simply the fear of not succeeding, and I will agree with him wholeheartedly. This affects my social as well as my private life. When meeting people I admire I will either back off and withdraw or come on entirely too strong. Seems like the more you fear something, the faster you bring it on yourself."

This young lady is suffering from a classic case of perfectionism. If a thing can't be done well, she prefers not to do it at all. To her, success and splendid achievement is everything, but trying something and learning from the experience, no matter how meager it might be, seem not to interest her at all. Because she makes success so extremely important, it eludes her constantly.

Take the case of Mr. Shera, a reasonably bright fellow who had been living on welfare most of his adult life. He started out being a tinsmith and was a reasonably good one, but never achieved the recognition and promotion he expected. Eventually he left and became a machinist. But this too was not as challenging as he wanted even though he could not be the best machinist in the shop after only two years. So he found himself longing for another field. And so it went for the first ten years of his married life and he found it more and more difficult to get jobs. Eventually he had to go on relief. The state rehabilitation office wanted to get him back as a productive individual and assigned him to psychotherapy—first with one therapist and then with another. Not one of them was able to budge the man into giving up his neurotic belief that working didn't pay off and that being on welfare was really easier than putting in a full eight-hour day.

When I saw him in counseling—the third and final attempt the rehabilitation office was willing to make—I had no more success than the others. I saw him as someone who had disciplined himself unusually hard to figure out how to stay out of work. Until he could change his attitude about having to be the best at whatever he was, he simply refused to play the game at all. He would not join a work force somewhere and simply do his best. As far as I was concerned his productive life was largely wasted because he was afraid of competing.

The major lesson to be learned is that *it is more important to do than to do well.* Stop playing God, stop insisting how good everything has to be that you attempt, and realize once and for all that everything has a beginning. You usually do badly in the beginning, and you are no different from anybody else. So start where you are and keep trying until you get better by *slow degrees.*

Another interesting example of how perfectionism

46

interferes with doing your best was shown in a study on intelligent and wealthy children. They had been told all their lives that they were different from other children and therefore did not need to demonstrate their superiority. Unfortunately this attitude created a sense of fear in the children that they might not live up to the high standards set by their parents, who thought that they were so perfect they couldn't make mistakes. Therefore, instead of performing their tasks with a sense of self-confidence and pleasure, they often avoided them completely or did them out of a fear that they would disappoint their parents. Self-discipline is enormously difficult under such conditions.

Betty is a girl who comes from a well-to-do family. Some of the members gained recognition at the universities where they worked and in state politics. She feels, therefore, that she has to live up to the high image set by her ancestors. Whatever she does must be done so well it cannot be criticized. Betty puts her heart and soul into her term papers, she looks up endless references, types the paper two or three times, and is so determined to make the thing a masterpiece that she runs out of time. At this point she asks her professor for an extension, which is often granted. But then she goes through the same neurotic search for perfection, again adding more references to her paper, rephrasing long paragraphs, and retyping it to a higher standard. Then when it is to be handed in she again finds a reason not to do so. She takes an incomplete in her course and adds this experience to several other incompletes. Eventually she has to leave school.

Betty then rationalizes that she didn't want to go to that particular school at all and didn't want to take that particular course. She then enrolls in another school, heading in another direction. But the same perfectionist and neurotic philosophies that she used in the past guide her in this new venture.

The sorry part of the tale is that Betty is a capable and intelligent person whose work could have earned her perfectly acceptable, if not outstanding, grades. Unfortunately Betty *had* to have A+'s or nothing at all. Instead of getting her work done and believing that *it is better to do than to do well,* she had the opposite philosophy, which is taught to millions of us: unless you can do something well, it shouldn't be done at all.

This philosophy is one of the most mistaken pieces of advice ever handed out to a generation of children. Stop and think for a moment how absurd the whole thing really sounds. If something cannot be done well, it should not be done at all—this is what it claims. Are we to suppose, therefore, that everything we do we must do well the first time? This is exactly what that philosophy suggests. Yet how is such a thing possible? If we did only those things which we do well, we would wind up sipping our soup and blowing our noses. Surely this cannot be taken seriously. It has always been recognized that man learns by trial and error. He frequently makes mistakes and if he learns from those mistakes, he can improve his performance until he discovers other mistakes. This process of trying something, regardless of whether it will be perfect or not, seeing which mistakes come forth and then correcting them, thereby permitting us to attempt the task again with this new insight, permits us to make progress. But this philosophy says that we should repeat only things that we do well, and anything that is done poorly should be forgotten.

The moral of this story is that it is not a disgrace to do

48

badly. As a matter of fact, it is *inevitable* that we do things badly when we first begin. It is part of the whole learning curve. It is impossible to learn things well right from the start unless they are extremely simple. All of our lives we have wrestled with tasks that seemed difficult at the time but now seem absurdly easy. It was not easy for us to learn to walk—we all fell many times. Talking came only laboriously—we slurred our words, repeated our sounds, mispronounced innumerable words. We did not learn how to use a knife and fork until we were well along into childhood. Learning to ride a bicycle was a painful experience; so was learning to swim. Even a chicken must learn how to peck for pieces of corn. It is not a skill that comes fully developed. That's right, chickens frequently miss the objects they are pecking at until they have had experience. If a chicken followed the advice that he should not peck unless he pecked accurately at all times, he would simply starve to death.

Therefore, those who insist on being perfect are bound to be the most imperfect. They will seldom accomplish their best, because they are shooting for the moon instead of some realistic goal here on earth. Those who want to play the role of superman will find that their all-too-human bodies simply do not equip them to be the best at everything. Most of us are not the best at anything. Yet life can still be beautiful, happy, and meaningful. But first we must get rid of the notion that it is terrible to play second fiddle, that we must always be number one, that we shouldn't do anything unless we can do it well, and other such nonsense. Vince Lombardi was one of the principal advocates of this particularly vicious piece of neuroticism. I think he said something like, "Winning isn't everything, it's the only

...ng." Losing can have it's pleasures too, unless you have some neurotic goal to be the best at all times. In my own experience I have enjoyed a great deal of activity when I was not being competitive and driving myself hard to win. When I didn't care about winning and just played for the fun of the game, I usually had a great deal more fun. Sometimes I won and sometimes I lost but I cared very little at the time. It was not a game to prove my perfection, it was a game to prove nothing except that one can have fun throwing a football or swimming or whatever.

If you are afraid to test yourself and to experience failure, stop rationalizing about why you are failing. The real reason is probably that you're simply afraid to face the fact that you are a human being who will not do well in everything. Finish what you are doing even though it will be a pretty sad product. Hand in your work and take your chances. Then try again on another task. Don't go through life starting something, getting it nearly completed, seeing that it is not a masterpiece, and then throwing it away. On the contrary, finish what you are doing, forget about having it perfect, and give yourself credit for at least trying.

It is more important to do than to do well. The main difficulty people have who are driven by perfection is that they have a faulty definition of success. To them success is doing something 100 percent okay and hardly anything less. It simply does not make sense to define success as near-perfection. Think of success rather as a slight bit of improvement over what you were able to do before. Even if you are trying something and do not see improvement, you are still entitled to say that you are improving, because the benefits of practice will show up later.

Suppose you were to break apart a boulder with a sledgehammer. It might require a great number of blows before the rock would fall apart, but you would not see any change in the rock until the very end. Does this mean that nothing was happening to the boulder before it shattered? Obviously hairline fractures were being created, and each blow of the hammer made these fractures just a bit bigger until finally the rock could no longer hold together.

The same applies to your behavior. As long as you are attempting something, improvement *is* being made. Even if your performance goes down, as it sometimes will, you can still learn from the experience. And that is the name of the game. If you play a piano piece more poorly today than you did yesterday, it doesn't mean that you have regressed. It could mean that you are trying the piece a new way, perhaps a bit faster, and therefore you are making more mistakes this time than you did before. But even this is an experience and will teach you to play better than you did before.

Therefore, whether you succeed or fail at something depends entirely upon your definition. Those who think they are failures all the time and feel dejected, depressed, and inferior have defined success as perfection. However, those who are optimistic about their behavior, who feel good about themselves, have simply defined success as reaching reasonable goals in little steps. It has never been an all-or-nothing thing with them.

Neurotic perfectionism is therefore impossible if you set your goals modestly, if you appreciate the fact that you are improving even when you see no improvement but are at least trying. Trying is the key word. Improvement comes if you try, *and* if you correct your next performance by what you learned from the previous trial.

Feelings of Inferiority

Good self-discipline is difficult for a person who feels inferior. For this reason I want to explain how we develop inferiority feelings and how to overcome them.

One of the basic misconceptions we have to deal with is the idea that *being inferior* and *feeling inferior* are the same. It is only when you *feel* inferior that you will allow life to defeat you. It is not when you happen *to be inferior* in some respect. Get rid of the idea that you should ever label yourself an "inferior person." There is no such thing as an inferior person. There are only persons who are inferior at particular skills. In other words, if I cannot run as fast as you, I am inferior to you as a runner. I am inferior to you as a singer if you reach higher or purer tones than I do. I am inferior to you as a dancer if all I can do is the fox-trot and you can do every conceivable step from the samba to the African hunting dance. In each of these respects I can fully admit that I am inferior to you but I never need to feel that I am an *inferior person* because of this. I am not talking about the *kind of people* we are, I am only talking about the kinds of traits we have. Some of my traits will be inferior to yours and undoubtedly some of yours will be inferior to mine. That has nothing to do with our worthiness as human beings. I don't need to judge *me* regardless of how many ways I am inferior to another human being to whom I am being compared. And the same of course applies to you. Therefore, it should not come as a surprise to anyone that each of us is inferior in many ways to everyone else depending upon which traits we are looking at. If you compare your skills to those of enough people, you will find that you are a great deal better than some and a great deal worse than others.

Most individuals seem to believe that they are worse than others only because they have been comparing themselves to persons who are usually a great deal better at a certain skill. It naturally must be concluded then that the person in question is inferior in all ways because he compares himself unfavorably most of the time.

For example, you might compare yourself to one of your friends who plays piano better than you do. Therefore you decide that this is another way in which you are inferior to everyone else. However, what you are ignoring is the fact that you are perhaps a better money earner than that person who plays the piano better. You may be a more stable person than that individual, you may have a broader appreciation of the arts, perhaps you are a healthier person. In fact, you might go on and on and begin to realize that in a great many ways you have a large number of traits in which you are superior. Unfortunately most of us do not take stock of ourselves this way. We usually pass judgment on ourselves on the basis of one or two traits and these are usually not our finest or our only ones.

Being inferior therefore only means that you are an imperfect human being who cannot be the best at everything. It is well to acknowledge the universal truth that in some respects you will outshine others and in other respects they will outshine you. That is all I am saying by the phrase "being inferior."

Feeling inferior is an entirely different story. When we feel that we are no good because we are, in fact, inferior in some respects, we are considering ourselves as good-for-nothing and worthless people who should be ashamed of ourselves. We run ourselves down and accept a subordinate position in life. We feel guilty, deserving of the worst treatment, all because we now believe that we are indeed bad, insignificant, and unimportant.

Feeling inferior is a gross neurotic act because you are judging yourself by your actions. You are saying, "I do things badly, therefore I am a bad and worthless person." This is the essence of the inferiority feeling. We judge ourselves by our actions, or, as Dr. Ellis says, we give ourselves report cards. If you want to overcome an inferiority feeling, stop equating your behavior with yourself. Stop judging yourself by your actions. Stop equating your strengths and weaknesses with yourself and *you will never feel inferior again.* And you may still have an enormous number of inferior traits.

Does this mean that if you were to admit your weaknesses, you would not do anything about them? Of course not. In fact, you might do a great deal more about your shortcomings if you had the courage to face them. Often people do not change their personalities and their shortcomings because they are ashamed to admit having them. If you cannot admit that you have a fault, how can you change it?

There are several reasons why you would be better off if you never rated yourself by your actions, traits, skills, or characteristics. You can do so if you like, of course, but you can't be logical about it at the same time.

1. *One characteristic can never describe all of you.*

People are enormously complex. They are a combination of many talents, behaviors, traits, and characteristics. One weakness among the lot does not cancel out the many strengths. The 97-pound weakling does not have the right to say he is inferior, since this totally ignores all his other merits and achievements. Perhaps he's a whiz at math or chess. Perhaps he's a very handsome youth, or has a great sense of humor, or is mature beyond his years. To suggest that he is inferior on the basis of that single quality (physical weakness) is simply absurd.

2. Many characteristics cannot describe all of you either.

"But why not?" you ask. "Isn't it possible to add up all my good points and all my bad points and see which I have more of?" I wish it were that simple, but it isn't.

For example, to add up all our merits and defects we'd first have to know how many merits we have and how many defects we have. But no one knows how many traits we have. The list could go on endlessly: there is honesty, charity, helpfulness, lightheartedness, easygoingness, pleasantness, industriousness, ambitiousness, and so on. Where does one stop? No one knows.

3. Our characteristics have never been scientifically weighted and cannot be averaged.

If you are going to take all the traits and skills there are in the world and judge yourself by them, we would first have to give each of them a value and then add up all these values and divide by the number of traits and skills to compute an average. Can we do that with any degree of agreement?

Is being miserly three times worse than being late? Or is it four times worse? Or a hundred times worse? Surely being mean toward one's children is more serious than occasionally being a few minutes late. But how much more serious? Who knows?

4. *Traits and skills do not remain constant.*

Suppose we could in fact agree upon a particular trait on which to rate you as a human being. And suppose that being a poor breadwinner makes you inferior. It would then make sense to judge you by that trait only as long as it did not change in quantity.

What, however, would happen to our thinking on this matter if you got a raise? Would you still be inferior? If you lost your job and were unemployed for a month, would you be more inferior than you were before? Then what would happen if you got a fine job after that and made twice as much money as you do currently? Would you then be half as inferior as you were before?

In other words, if the trait is not constant, then how can we judge your inferiority as a constant trait? If it is going up and down like a yo-yo, my idea of your inferiority would go up and down like a yo-yo too. It would be the same as my trying to measure a desk that is made of a material which changes size constantly. I might find that it is six feet in length in the morning but seven and one half feet at night. If you should ever ask me what the length of the desk was, I would be hard pressed to tell you unless it would be only for the moment.

Desks do not behave this way of course, but human traits do. If you were to judge me as a tennis player, for example, you would be constantly changing your mind since I am fair at tennis one day but poorer the next. Therefore, how can I judge myself by a talent that never stands still?

5. *Who is to decide which traits and skills we should judge ourselves by?*

Suppose that we did have a constant trait and that it was a single one. Who is there in this world who could determine for me which trait I should use in order to judge myself? And who, frankly, is there in this world who could make that judgment? Should I judge for you because I am a clinical psychologist? But I am only human and I may not know you as well as you know yourself. Do you want to leave this up to your friend, your minister, your teacher, your psychotherapist? You know full well that all of us will not agree, so whose opinion should you accept? Well then, if we shouldn't use others to make these determinations, then why not ourselves? Simply because we aren't the same from moment to moment either. Since we are changing all the time, the way we feel about our skills changes also. At one time we are very bitter at ourselves because we do badly at something and on another day we don't seem to mind it at all. It does not make sense, therefore, to suggest that there is actually a person in this world who can tell us which traits we should judge ourselves by.

Summary

It appears that the argument against judging ourselves by our abilities and traits simply comes down to this: We are not being rational or sensible in the slightest when we judge ourselves, because (a) our traits constantly change; (b) there is no way of agreeing as to what is good or bad behavior at all times; (c) we cannot judge ourselves on one piece of behavior; (d) we never know how many other behaviors we should include before we judge ourselves; and (e) we will never agree as to who is qualified to make these judgments even if the above objections could be removed.

This leaves us with one simple conclusion: *Never judge yourself at all.* Judge your behavior if you like, but not yourself. You and your actions are not the same for the reasons I have demonstrated above. If you bear this point in mind, you may comfortably admit any number of faults from now on, but you will not feel like an inferior person merely because you are inferior *in certain respects.* It is always important to remember those last three words of the preceding sentence—in certain respects. That is what this whole business really boils down to.

If you can get over the idea of ever feeling inferior again, you will find enormous energy released from your body and brain to devote to the task of doing what you like in this life and making the most of it. Then, when you fail in what you are doing, even when you are applying good discipline, you will not feel worthless. Rather, you will get right back on your feet and apply yourself to the task anew without ever raising the question at all of how worthwhile you are as a person.

There are no inferior people, only inferior behaviors. Since we have no right to judge ourselves or others by behavior, we have no right to condemn ourselves or others.

4
Techniques of
Self-Discipline

Take Risks: The Secret of Self-Confidence

Fear is one of those emotions which frequently root us to inaction. Achievement becomes impossible as long as you are so scared that you won't try the task you fear. To overcome this obstacle you will need to question two irrational beliefs: (1) It would be a catastrophe if you were to engage in that feared task again, and (2) It is easier to avoid a difficult task than it is to face it.

Karen was on the high school swim team. Once, during a race, she swallowed water, coughed, lost her breath, went under for a few seconds, and lost the race. Thereafter, every so often she became so tense about swimming (especially competitive swimming) that she developed rapid breathing until she felt dizzy and had to be fished out of the pool. By the time her parents brought the girl for counseling she was ready to give up racing altogether.

My task was to reduce her fear enough so that she could get back into the swim and gradually relax again in the water. First, I had her question why it was so terribly serious if she did hyperventilate in the water.

Would she really drown, with dozens of spectators watching her every move? Couldn't she flip over and float to the pool's edge if she felt dizzy? Would people laugh at her, and, if so, couldn't she really tolerate it?

Secondly, I urged her to do *more* swimming, to risk more feats rather than to avoid them, regardless of how difficult that might be at first. I wanted her to question her neurotic philosophy that avoiding difficult situations was easier than facing them. Unless she took a number of risks, however difficult, she would establish a habit of running away from frightening things. That would cause the fear to spread to other activities, and before long she would find life mighty dull.

We had two sessions on these themes, and several weeks later I received a note from her parents telling me that she was back swimming races, no longer terrified of shortness of breath and feeling self-confident again.

The life that has no risk in it is not worth living. Do what you want to learn, don't watch from the sidelines. In the *doing* we learn what works or what doesn't work. Don't waste your time fooling yourself that you'll give speeches as soon as you're better at giving them. You're not going to get better unless you actually speak in public. You can watch orators all day long and you won't learn as much as giving a five-minute address to the P.T.A. can teach you. Why? Because we learn best when we practice a skill.

This may sound quite obvious and you'll insist that everybody knows this, but I doubt it. Aren't there goals you've wanted to achieve but haven't because you have never attempted them? Maybe you want to dance superbly but are embarrassed at your present clumsiness. My advice? Get on the dance floor with all your clumsiness and dance, dance, dance at every opportunity until you improve.

"But," you may protest, "what's wrong with watching others for a while first and then trying my hand at it? Wouldn't I avoid some embarrassment that way?"

You might, to be sure. But watching for a short while only is all that would do you any good. Sooner or later you'll have to get on the floor and actually see for yourself what your faults are.

Parents who refuse to allow their children to learn the hard way end up with kids who have little self-confidence and poor self-discipline. If your teen-age daughter wants to bake a cake, don't deny her the opportunity. You know that she may burn a pan, her cake may fall, the kitchen may be a mess. Some dishes may be broken. But, do you want her to learn to bake? Then let her start *doing* it. She can watch you for a month of Sundays and learn practically nothing. *It is more important to do than to do well.* The second time she tries to bake a cake she'll probably remember her mistakes from her first effort. The second trial may still be a mess, to be sure, but if she tries it often enough, she'll learn to bake just as you learned—by trial and error.

Do you want children with self-confidence and a minimum of inferiority feelings? Then never discourage them from trying anything that is not foolishly dangerous. Sure they'll do terribly at it. *That's why they should be urged to do it.* Stop showing them over and over the way you knit, change a tire, play a passage on the piano, or bake a soufflé. Once or twice is enough. Then hope they want to try for themselves.

A researcher did a study illustrating this very point. He had one group of children watch a mechanical puzzle being assembled, after which they tried to repeat the process. It took them sixteen trials on the average to learn the secret.

He let another group try the puzzle first, then corrected their errors by demonstration. This second method took 25 percent fewer trials than the first. Clearly, watching a task is usually not enough to create rapid learning. You must *do* what you want to learn.

Risk-taking was never demonstrated to me more dramatically as a source of growth than in the case of Richard. He came from a professional family but dropped out of high school in chase of a rainbow assortment of drugs. My job was to encourage him to get his diploma so he could begin his college studies.

I quickly and easily determined that he was afraid of failure. Despite my reminding him time after time that it is more important to do than to do well, he still did not decide to take his final test until I pushed the phone on my desk across to him and told him to make the appointment. A week later he passed the test, much to the amazement of his family and himself.

But to get his diploma he still needed to pass the test on the constitutions of both America and Illinois. He said he'd study an hour a day for a week and then take that test too. I questioned him at our next session and discovered that he had canceled the test because he was not ready. I had him make another appointment to take the test and urged him to study thirty minutes a day for the week.

At the following therapy session he again admitted that he hadn't touched the books and would not be taking the test. I could hardly believe the fear he must have had. Richard had always been told he had to do everything perfectly and so it was easy to understand why he was so chickenhearted when he had to risk failure. I decided that he had to be pushed harder, so I picked up the phone, gave his name as the caller, and made an appointment for him to take the test in thirty minutes. When I hung up he felt the pressure and came out with the classic rationalization of all time: "I can't take that test today. It's my birthday."

After some reminders that *taking* the test was more important than passing it, he decided to cooperate. He began to appreciate that he'd learn what the test was like, what he would have to study if he had to repeat the test, and what *not* to study. I gave him a broad smile, slapped him on the shoulder repeating the two secrets of good self-discipline: (1) It is easier to face a difficult task than to avoid it, and (2) It is more important to do than to do well.

I heard later that afternoon that—miracle of miracles—Richard had passed the test, paid his five dollars, and took home his high school diploma. He was overjoyed at that unexpected birthday gift.

That is how self-confidence is developed. You take a chance, you learn something from your attempt—even if it's only what *not* to do next time—and you use that knowledge in your next trial. That's not failure. It's gradual success and that's impossible without risk-taking.

You never fail as long as you are trying. Each trial teaches you something if you study your behavior. You're getting valuable feedback from each effort, and this information is a small segment of success. Don't knock it. If you repeat the trials often enough, you add up little successes on top of little successes until they become noticeable. The upshot is that you are failing *only* when you are not trying, never otherwise.

Fight the Fear of Being Phony

Some people cannot bring themselves to act sociably because they think they come across like a phony back-slapping salesman, politician, or social climber. If coming up to an acquaintance and using his first name, asking him about the wife and kids, and inquiring into his health embarrasses you because you feel insincere, do it until you feel sincere. Your reaction is not an indication of phoniness, only newness. How could you expect to be comfortable with behavior you've never seriously pursued?

A young executive from New York felt self-conscious and even guilty when he spoke with an accent. He didn't like his native Bronx speech but felt so phony speaking any other way that he couldn't discipline himself to give it up.

Another person who had always lived modestly found it most uncomfortable to wear expensive suits, join the local athletic club, get his hair trimmed at chic men's shops, wouldn't wear rings, use hair sprays, or body deodorants. The whole effect was so out of keeping with the down-to-earth vision he always had of himself that he became painfully self-conscious when trying to break out of the old mold.

He too confused newness with sham. Surely he was pretending to be sophisticated and slick when he really wasn't. So what? How do you learn anything unless you try? Being a phony for a while is the price you pay for change. If you keep it up, the day will surely come when you will feel more and more comfortable in your new role until the thought of being a phony is completely overcome.

What's so great about our *not* changing, anyway? Should every hillbilly forever talk with his hill twang? Shouldn't you want to enlarge your vocabulary? What if some people think you're putting on airs if you use a literary vocabulary instead of street jargon? Talking like an English professor is bound to raise eyebrows at first, and you're certain to be uncomfortable as you try to speak like a knowledgeable and educated person. But look at the result!

Unless the fear of being insincere is overcome, a waitress will never aspire to be a movie star and be presented to the queen. The young executive will never reach the executive suite if he doesn't play the role expected of an aspiring leader. In short, what you call phony is, in my view, nothing more than a pair of shoes that need breaking in.

Earn the Reward

Some years ago I read of a uranium prospector who practiced a strict form of self-discipline that was largely responsible for his becoming a millionaire.

He set himself goals. He would walk a specific number of miles before he'd allow himself the luxury of resting; climb that curious bluff before he permitted himself another drink of water; not stop for dinner until he had taken a certain number of samples. In this way, he drove himself from one immediate goal to another until he could look back with satisfaction at the end of the day at the ground he had explored.

This is the same technique I have used in writing these very pages. I started out this morning flying to the East Coast. Before permitting myself to look at a news magazine, I determined to write some notes for a lawyer who would be questioning me. Then, as a reward, I read several articles and wrote a letter to my mother. I returned to the magazine for a few more articles and then decided to write all that I could on this book until I arrived back home. However, after finishing each subheading of the preceding pages, I set the pad aside and conversed with a passenger or ate a meal. Sometimes I rewarded myself with looking out of the window but not until I had completed a section. *Then* I felt free to indulge in relaxation.

"Isn't this being hard-nosed?" you may ask. Of course it is. But if you want to reach an end point, you've got to do what it takes, that's all. I want to finish this book. Unless I make myself get down to brass tacks and do it, I'll never see its completion. Too bad that I can't do this *and* read all I like, or converse with people all I like, or watch the scenery all I like. The long and the short of it is that I can't have it both ways. Tough. So I plug along reaching a short-range goal, rewarding myself, reaching another goal, rewarding myself. With my hard-nosed attitude, I can see with pleasure that I have sixteen handwritten pages today that I didn't have before.

This technique leads naturally to the next one.

Work First, Then Play

In a manner of speaking, every undisciplined person is really a playboy or a playgirl at heart. What you are saying when you put pleasure before responsibility is that you can't stand to face responsibilities. You have to be pleased all the time, always have pleasure in your life. Work is so horrible that it must be put aside always and must never stand in the way of fun and games.

This is hardly the way to become self-disciplined. The

66

much wiser philosophy is to *get the work done first* and then enjoy yourself. This accomplishes two things: first, the job gets done; and secondly, you are able to enjoy your fun free of guilt and free of nagging thought that you still have to go back and finish what you avoided. For example, if you run off to a movie in the evening before doing the dishes, you simply will not enjoy the movie as much as if you had done them first. You'll spoil the movie by recalling what you have to do when you arrive home, how late it will be, how sticky the food will be when you finally get to scraping the plates at ten or eleven at night, and how you wish you had done it all before you left. These unpleasant thoughts are bound to draw from the pleasure you could have experienced if you had taken in the movie totally free of any extraneous concerns.

This philosophy of putting work before pleasure is also a fine technique for getting a great many other things done. For example, suppose you have been wanting to buy yourself a pair of shoes. You know that you tend to be extravagant and that you buy things before you really need them. Then face the responsibility of wearing out the old shoes first, and promise yourself that you will not get a new pair until you really need them. Or if you desire to read a book on the weekend and you must mow the lawn, do the work first. Get the lawn mowed and then reward yourself for that responsible act by sitting down quite carefree and read whatever you like. If you begin reading your favorite mystery first, you could become so absorbed in it that the grass never gets cut and you will have three times more difficulty with it when you finally get to it.

Therefore, if you want to diet or exercise, do not allow yourself other pleasures until these duties are taken care of. Do not accept any phone calls, for example, until you have done your exercises. Do not allow yourself to watch television or have a cup of coffee until the living room is picked up. Get your bedroom done first before you have a coffee klatch with the neighbor. Write your bills before you go next door to socialize. You will find life becoming easier for you, frustrations kept at a minimum, things getting done fairly effortlessly—all because you have decided to put work before pleasure.

You Have an Enemy: Your Neurosis

When you can't convince yourself to knuckle down to a difficult task, remember that you have an enemy in this world who is out to do you in. This enemy rejoices in your goofing off and wants you to be as unproductive as possible. He relishes the fact that you will fail, that you are afraid, and that you are not getting anywhere in life. This enemy is chuckling over your unused talents and also because you are not getting the satisfactions that all of your potential is screaming for.

That enemy is your neurosis. Your neurosis states that it hurts less to goof off than it does to put your shoulder to the wheel. Your neurosis tells you that you are better off to avoid failure and rejection even though it will cost you boredom and pain.

Tommy was one of those people who would not work because he was afraid of doing badly. He felt inadequate and was often bored with his job. He even developed stomach pains and finally thought people were talking about him. He used all these excuses as reasons for not going to work. This is how his neurotic problem finally conquered him.

68

He thought he would have less pain staying home and having these ailments than going on the job and being bored or perhaps fired. But none of those things he feared were nearly as bad as the ones he experienced by not disciplining himself. That is the point to bear in mind. You would never sit still for one moment if someone made you suffer the way you are making yourself suffer. If you did, you'd regard that person as the meanest and cruelest individual you had ever encountered. How could anyone deliberately deny you your talent? What kind of inhuman beast would make you stay at home all day watching television and wonder what was happening in the world? What kind of torturer would make your stomach hurt the way yours does? Who is this enemy that you despise? Who is this enemy that is ruining your life? Hold on to your hat. It is you! It is your neurotic belief that the pain you suffer by risk-taking and facing your difficulties is less than the pain you suffer if you don't. That is the mistake. You will probably be uncomfortable either way, whether you face your problems or don't. But you will be *less* disturbed if you face them. Don't be your own worst enemy. There are enough people in the world who will give you a bad time, so don't be the biggest headache you have. Get after this internal enemy, this fellow who totally disrespects you. Throw him out!

I remember well a young girl who had failed her driver's test five or six times. At the time I saw her she had very little confidence and was certainly not about to take another driver's test. She was humiliated because she was a college graduate. It was quite apparent to me why she failed. Her nerves were so easily set off that the mere thought of taking a test sent her into a tailspin. For this reason I immediately recommended that she go back and take the test again and again and again until she did pass it. But in order to do that I had to convince her that failure and rejection by people who might laugh at her for this was really not horrible. First of all, she really could not point to anyone who rejected her, and she certainly could not demonstrate that having failed the test was a catastrophic event. It simply meant that she would have to accept rides from others, take buses, or walk. This in fact she had been doing for a couple of years.

As a result of the "horrible" thing she made of taking the test again she told herself that it was easier to avoid it than it would be to face it, and therefore nothing happened. I urged her to take the test again and surprisingly enough she passed.

This is only an example of the kinds of things all of us are confronted with all the time. It is the fear of doing badly or the fear of rejection that makes us so cowardly even discipline won't help. For one person it may be telling jokes in company; for another the painful event may be giving a speech in public. I have known some persons with all the confidence in the world who could sell peace pipes to the Indians but who would never invite anyone into their homes for dinner. Some people who are able to be the most gracious hostesses refuse to dress up foolishly for a costume ball. I have known men who felt perfectly at ease in company, and yet were terrified at the possibility of making important decisions. Each of us in our own way defines what is horrible in our life and then we avoid it like the plague.

To overcome your fears, therefore, and to allow yourself to become more self-disciplined, examine carefully those two neurotic attitudes which always cause anxiety, worry, fear, and panic: (1) Something is terrible, horrible, catastrophic, the end of the world, and (2) I must think about this all the time, focus on it, dwell upon it, and never let it out of my mind. If you entertain either or both of these ideas, you are going to be afraid, and no amount of logical talk about self-discipline is going to have much effect on you. To employ self-discipline you must always work at becoming a risk-taking person. It does not hurt to be risk-taking unless the risk is foolish and dangerous. How can it hurt to be rejected by someone? Or not to do things perfectly? These are the kinds of risks I strongly advocate that you take. Today or tomorrow do something that you have been wanting to do all your life. Don't put it off. Take the risk and see what happens. And then, if at all possible, stay with it until you are able to do it.

Limit Your Goals

Some people find it hard to discipline themselves because they undertake too many things at one time. This saps their strength, distracts them from the intense concentration that is often necessary in order to achieve something. It demands the impossible by expecting more hours in the day than there are. If, for example, you want to write a book, paint a picture, learn a language, play bridge, and take care of your house on weekends, you may find that there is so little time that you can never achieve any of them.

To write a book, for example, requires more than a few minutes a day. And the same is true for painting a picture, cleaning the house, and so on. You can conceivably do a hundred different tasks in one day if you spend about three and a half minutes on each of them. But then it might take you a hundred years to get these jobs done. This is entirely unsatisfactory and does not really give pleasure to life.

It is much wiser to limit ourselves to a few important tasks and let the matter go at that. Generally try to finish one job before you take on another. Or at least never have more than several goals at one time because you will not be able to focus on them adequately. In other words, don't try to diet and stop smoking at the same time. If you can do that, well and good. But in all likelihood one job at a time is plenty. Or don't try to work forty hours a week and take on a full college course. Most people will simply collapse under the weight of such a program. Either cut back on the job, or the course work, or both. And don't at the same time try to undertake a golf tournament on the weekends unless, of course, you're exceptional. Then, by all means, push yourself to the limit.

I have often heard it said, "You can do anything if you want to." This is totally false on two counts. First, you may not have the talents to do all the things that you would enjoy: being an opera singer, a baseball player, a high diver, and so on. If you are tone deaf, poorly coordinated, and have a fear of height, you are simply never going to be able to do them no matter how much you might want to.

But secondly, to do all these things requires so much time that you simply cannot pursue them all at once. When you stop to think about it, it takes about four years to learn to play the piano fairly respectably. Painting probably takes that long as well. Most people cannot write a book in less than several months. Building a house takes many months. And these time spans will certainly not allow for excellence. If you really put your heart and soul into any of these tasks, their completion could literally require many years. If this is the case, then how are you to find time for many such activities?

Babe Didrikson was a fantastic athlete who was apparently outstanding in every athletic endeavor she undertook. But even she knew that she had to take up one thing at a time. She didn't swim vigorously in the morning, ski in the afternoon, and fence at night. That would have been too confusing and could have caused conflicts in her whole physical and neurological system. When she decided to go into one sport she tended to exclude others until she had that one mastered. For example, when she decided to learn golf, she worked at that in the morning before she went to work and in the evening after she returned from work. Then she often put in fourteen to sixteen hours a day on weekends until her hands were blistered. There was no time for serious effort in any other sport. Where would the time have come from?

And this is the point I make. We cannot excel at a number of things unless we have tunnel vision. We must have a single-mindedness of purpose that says, "This is the thing I want to do and I am not going to let anything else come in my way." If you want to graduate from college or from graduate school, you had better remind yourself constantly that these goals are not only important but they are the *most* important pursuits of your life for the time being. Do not let other things distract you. You have no time for other jobs. You have no time for marriage. Remember, you cannot do a number of complex things well and at the same time. Confine yourself to a few goals but devote yourself to them. Then when you have reached a point that satisfies you, drop that program and pick up another. Then start all over again, being careful not to spread yourself too thinly.

Don't Let Slips Add Up

If you are in the process of breaking the cigarette habit and you decide one night to have just one, realize what you are letting yourself in for. The moment you allow yourself to have "just one" cigarette, to break the habit one time, it becomes a little bit easier to take the second. And when you have had two cigarettes it becomes easier to take a third one. Slips add up.

This sounds so self-evident that it is not worth mentioning. However, it is vitally important. You will have to keep it in mind if you ever want to learn to be fully self-disciplined. Do not allow the first slip to take place and you will not have to worry about the second and the third and the thousandth.

One of my clients had been trying to discipline himself to jog once a day. He kept this up for some months and felt very good about it. However, he was ill with the flu for a short time and could not jog for three days in a row. He saw this as no threat to his habit, so he was immediately back on the streets on the fourth day. But then the attractiveness of not doing it got to him because he remembered how nice it was not to jog on a cold winter night. Therefore one night he was not exactly up to it, and when the weather was a bit uncomfortable, he decided to let it go for that one night, promising himself to make up for it. And this he did. But several weeks after that he found himself again making excuses and he again skipped jogging. This continued intermittently until, in a matter of several months, he was down to jogging only once or twice a week and faltering seriously on his whole athletic program.

These little slips are like drugs. You start off small but in order to get the same effect, you simply have to keep on taking larger and larger doses. Allowing yourself to goof off once can be so tempting that the second time becomes easier, and so forth.

Therefore one of the greatest deterrents against developing poor self-discipline is simply not to let that first slip take place. If you do, then redouble your efforts to remain disciplined. Once you start to slide, it is difficult to reverse direction. Why let yourself lose all the ground you gained and then have to work back laboriously when a little effort each time is all it takes to keep the habit going vigorously?

In my own life I can see how easily the tendency to ignore little slips eventually leads to major modifications in my behavior patterns. If I do not regularly use dental floss every night, because I am tired one night or make excuses that night, I find it awfully easy not to do it the following night and to accept another excuse several days later when I may be tired or distracted. The same goes for brushing my teeth, exercising, or doing a certain amount of reading every day.

To fight this insidious process you need to understand why it works so well. When you indulge yourself you experience immediate pleasure. This pleasure may be so satisfying that you find it hard to compete with frustrating yourself and then being pleased days or weeks later. Therefore, if you allow yourself to taste that fleeting pleasure once, you are obviously quite tempted to do it again and again. That's why disciplining oneself is usually so hard: you are fighting against a whole series of immediate rewards that are in competition with immediate frustrations and *later* rewards. But if you keep in mind that later rewards are often more beneficial than the immediate ones, you will find it less difficult to discipline yourself.

Nibble at Big Tasks

One of the biggest obstacles to getting people to stay with a task comes from looking at the enormous amount of work that must be done and being overwhelmed by it. The tasks we undertake, such as four years of college, four years of graduate school, ten years of building a business, years to learn a language, to learn how to play the piano, and a hundred other endeavors, all look overwhelming when we see what is in store for us. If you have this outlook, you will probably not undertake much, because you cannot help feeling overwhelmed.

Instead, I strongly suggest that you break your goals into thousands of smaller ones. Then take one goal at a time. Nibble away at a mountain of cheese—that's what a mouse does. It is amazing how much can be done if you simply take a little bit at a time and stay with it day after day after day until the thing is finally done. I was once told that it is possible to read the complete works of Shakespeare in one year if only fifteen minutes a day are devoted to it. Fifteen minutes a day can be set aside by practically anyone even if it is only while sitting on the john and perhaps also just before retiring. Reading a ten-volume set of the story of civilization is entirely possible if you simply decide to spend a certain amount of time on it every day. You will be amazed at how chapters will fly by. Perhaps in a couple of years you will have read the whole series. If you have to spade up your garden, don't despair simply because it is large. Break it up into small segments and decide to do a segment every day or every week. Then follow the plan regularly and before you know it the whole job will be done. I once had to bring the contents of a whole filing cabinet full of folders to my home and thought of hiring a truck to do the job. Instead, I took half a dozen folders home with me every night for about three months and, without any effort, had the entire mass of folders nicely transferred to my basement without any strain or expense.

Do you want to paint your house but haven't the time? Of course you have the time if you are willing to take a long time to do it. Set aside a certain number of boards that you will do every evening after work. Or decide to do what you can in one hour. Then wash out your brush and enjoy life as usual. Next day do the same thing. Then assign yourself to do one window an evening and perhaps two windows and a door on a weekend. In this way you will find that you are able to achieve an enormous amount of work because you are constantly at it and the work is never a strain or a pressure.

In this day and age we tend to think that we must always work rapidly, we must always achieve as though we are on an assembly line in a factory. In fact, some of the greatest works of art have been done laboriously and slowly, taking years and decades. Pyramids were built a stone at a time, the Roman highway system was laid brick by brick, and every great painting was done a stroke at a time, all taking many years.

I am never particularly overwhelmed when I decide to write a book. I deliberately break it into small segments so that I never feel intimidated by it. All I require is fifteen minutes or half an hour between appointments, enough time to give me an opportunity to organize my notes a bit, put my feet up on my desk, and dictate. One section at a time, separated by several days, and this procedure followed for several months, easily produces a book.

I shall never forget the way in which I wrote the first book of this series, *Overcoming Depression.* I decided to allot myself the time I would ordinarily spend watching television commercials. My office was adjacent to the recreation room, and for the length of time a television commercial was on I would type what I had outlined. This enabled me to do about one page a night. Then on weekends I would type ten pages, giving me fifteen pages a week. The entire book was about a hundred and fifty pages long, which meant that ten weeks was all that it took, and I was never under any strain whatever. Of course, additional time was required to do the rewriting and polishing. However, this too was done on an allotted and rationed basis. It could be done easily, without great strain, and yet done effectively.

How does a mouse eat a mountain of cheese? A nibble at a time. If he rations himself certain amounts every day, the time will obviously and inevitably come when he will be out of cheese. The same applies to any task you face.

Keep Disciplined Company

Another technique for developing good discipline is to make sure that you are in the company of people who are disciplined also. Nothing can eat away at your resolve more quickly than someone who is always giving in to his pleasures and tempting you with all that you are fighting against.

This is especially bothersome and even unfortunate when that other person happens to be your spouse. I recall particularly the case of a couple who once came to me who really were quite miserable with each other although they were very much in love. The major problem seemed to be that they were simply not good for each other because neither one was very disciplined. If the husband suggested they buy something that was way beyond their means, the wife usually went right along with this and offered no resistance. As a result they were continually fighting off bill collectors and living in such a whirlwind of robbing Peter to pay Paul that life was really not too pleasant in the long run.

This collusion between husband and wife, this marriage of two undisciplined people, had its unhappy effects in many other ways. Their home was in constant disorder, the children were frequently ignored, the teachers tried to control the children but they got no support from either of the parents because each was as undisciplined as the other.

It is literally amazing how much easier it is to diet if your mate will diet with you. Or if you want to stop smoking and your mate will break the habit along with you, then you have that social support which makes the job so much easier. Or if you are thinking of buying a new car that is totally impractical for you and you have a mate who says "No," it is easier to avoid the trap of satisfying yourself with short-range goals. The mere presence of someone else giving you a different viewpoint or disagreeing with your action is frequently enough to give you the time to rethink your plan and to come up with a better one. So if you can form a club to work on some common goal, go to it. It makes enormously good sense psychologically. But short of that, let me encourage you always to travel in circles with people who do what they say they will do, who can control their liquor and their food intake, and who have attained some measure of success simply by sheer willpower. Being around them almost assures that some of their willpower will rub off on you. If you do this, you won't be in the predicament the Smiths were in one Christmas when they both let their buying of presents run into hundreds of dollars, an amount they couldn't afford. They literally could not replenish their food for several days thereafter. This may evoke a chuckle, but I assure you the Smiths were disgusted with their own lack of foresight and their inability to control themselves.

Be a Stoic

I do not think it is possible to be a well-disciplined person unless you learn to be a stoic. This means you must develop the mental attitude whereby you can endure pain, misery, unhappiness, and all kinds of frustrations. If you cave in on your goals every time you don't like what is happening, and if you back away simply because you are experiencing discomfort, I guarantee that you won't get most of what you want and you will never be well disciplined. Good self-discipline and suffering go hand in hand. The whole point of this book, however, is to insist that the suffering you endure as a stoic is less than the suffering you have if you are not.

Judy was a girl with a history of failure despite the fact that she had only one year to go to finish college. Unfortunately her money had run out, but if she had found employment and saved, she might have accumulated enough funds to return to college to finish her education. When I proposed that she do precisely this her answer was, "But I can't find anything but boring jobs."

"So what?"

"You don't understand. You oversimplify. It isn't that easy just to take on a boring job. I can't stand to work eight hours a day at something I don't like."

"Nonsense. You *can* stand it, but you *won't*. If you want to accept reality, then you have to realize that the only way you are going to finish college, in all likelihood, is for you to work at a boring job. So what? It is hardly going to kill you, but you think it will. Therefore you avoid it like the plague and then you get nowhere. You don't seem to understand the necessity of suffering with *some pain now* in exchange for *much less pain later.* The discomfort, the frustration, the unhappiness that go with working are not unbearable things, they are just regrettable ones."

Around and around we went, and I can't even recall at this point whether she finally accepted my advice or not. I suspect, however, that she simply went on as she always had, though there had to be something else explaining her behavior rather than that she was simply unwilling to put up with some displeasure.

I recall another woman who was engaged for several years but the relationship never really advanced to the point where she wanted to marry him. She always hoped he would change, and it was quite apparent that he would not. When she was questioned in some detail as to why she could not break off the engagement, it turned out that she would be alone and would have to start over with a new relationship and this would be painful. It was again the fear of willingly walking into a painful situation for the present that made her suffer much more in the three-year period. Had she broken the engagement three years before, she might by now have been happily married or at least have found someone new.

Another woman had wanted for five years to leave her husband. She rationalized that she would feel guilty about hurting him, and was annoyed over making her mother's prediction come true that she was a fool for entering a marriage which would never work out. To prove her mother wrong she was willing to endure that relationship all those years just so her mother couldn't snicker at her and say, "I told you so."

Again, in her case the real reason she was afraid was the pain of being embarrassed. She thought she could not have endured it. Why cannot people endure pain? They do anyway. It is just that they don't enjoy it and certainly don't ask for it. The reason they often behave so unwisely is that they are in such a haste to get away from pain that they cause more of it. Sometimes it is a great deal wiser to recognize that your move is going to be a painful one, but that in the long run it is the least painful of the options you have. However, only a philosophy of stoicism, a need sometimes to suffer in this world, can provide this. As it ironically turns out, *those people who are prepared to suffer do the least suffering.* It is those who are always running away from pain who receive the greatest amount of suffering. The two cases cited above are clear examples of this. The one woman endured an engagement that was never going to materialize into marriage and the second one lived in an unhappy marriage that was never going to improve. But to avoid certain discomforts they went on year after year, suffering endlessly more than they needed to if they had simply made one final and painful decision: to break off that relationship.

Be a stoic. Bear pain gracefully. This is the price you often have to pay to make significant changes for the better.

Time Yourself

One of the most discouraging features about doing a task is to believe the job will take so long that it has to be overwhelming and therefore is to be avoided. You can't mow the lawn, because you don't have enough time left in the afternoon. You haven't changed the oil in your car, because you have to get dressed for a party soon. The kitchen needs painting, but you haven't found a completely free weekend.

In this way, we tend to put things off until that wonderful day when we have a whole morning or a whole day absolutely free.

This simply is not necessary. If you will learn to time yourself on tasks, you may be amazed to find out how little time it takes to do the things you have been putting off. For example, mowing my lawn takes an hour and a half at the most. It takes a couple of evenings to paint a kitchen. Oil can be changed in less than an hour. Get into the car, drive it to the station, have the oil drained, and drive home in time for your party.

Time after time in the writing of this book I ran into the same problem. When I had ten minutes of free time I thought it would be nice if I could complete another few pages, but what could I accomplish in ten minutes? Then I decided to time myself to see how long it would take to complete one of the subheadings. Much to my surprise it was only a matter of a few minutes' dictation. Ten minutes was much more than I usually needed. Thereafter I was better prepared to tackle another section when I had a few minutes available. It was in this way that much of the book was done. I simply pulled out the slips of paper on which I had notes and in that brief time dictated the material at my leisure.

The next time you want to clean up your basement, time yourself accurately. Make a mental note or keep an actual record of the time. Then, when you have that job to do again, you will know how long it took and you will be most surprised to learn that in all likelihood you can not only clean the basement but probably shovel the snow from the driveway, wash the car, or read ten pages of your favorite novel.

Go While You're Hot

There are times when you have to push yourself like the very dickens to get a job done. Your heart is not in it and you would rather be doing a thousand other things. But you also know that unless you keep your nose to the grindstone, your projects will not advance. So you do it against all inner inclinations. You consider the whole matter drudgery, and hope the time will come when you feel more inspired and joyful about your task.

Happily, if you keep this up, the time *will* come when you will be inspired again. It is then that you want to put every ounce of energy behind your mission while the energy lasts. When you're hot, that's when you want to move. Do not let a period of inspiration go by without taking full advantage of it. These periods only come every so often, and they only last just so long. Therefore when you have such a piece of luck, use it to the fullest and you will be able to accomplish tenfold during those periods what you could otherwise.

For example, you have been assigned a certain number of books to read and you suddenly get this period of inspiration. Take advantage of it and read as many as you can while that energy lasts. Read before you go to bed, read after lunch, read on weekends, read on the bus or the subway, make full use of the drive that you have, knowing full well that one of these days you are going to get tired of this and won't want to keep up that pace. When that happens you may want to stay with your task but you will accomplish less with a lot more effort. But it will be comforting to look back and see what you accomplished during that peak period.

The same can be said for selling, working around the house, or whatever. When you hit it hot as a salesman, don't stop with just a few sales. Really go and make hay while the sun shines. Or in regard to doing chores around the house, after you get one done, don't just sit back and enjoy it. Clean the screens, paint the back porch, nail down the roof, mow the lawn, replace those two shrubs in the front yard.

This is how some people get an enormous amount of work done. They capitalize on that beautiful moment of inspiration, that period of great drive, and they suck every piece of energy out of it that it can give.

Burn Your Bridges

How often have you committed yourself to do something and when the going got tough you gave in and retreated? And how important was the fact that you had a place to retreat to? Now suppose you felt pushed against the wall, with no other place to go. The situation had you in a corner. Where then could you go except forward? See the point I'm driving at? When you have to do something, burn your bridges behind you so that you cannot rationalize your way back to where you started. Then you have no choice but to plow forward for better or worse and to complete the thing you started.

Stalin did this once when the Russians were in a battle against the Germans. He literally had the bridges burned so that the army simply had to stand its ground and fight for its very life. The Russians won, due, in no small measure, I believe, to the fact that it was either fight or die.

In the beginning pages of this book I mentioned the man who climbed Mt. Blanc. Apparently one of the most propelling forces that made him face the difficulty was his having committed himself to so many people that he simply couldn't back out. He had deliberately told his friends, his business associates, and everyone whom he respected that he was going to make that climb. Once having committed himself so thoroughly, it would have been extremely awkward to have backed out. There was some wisdom in his deliberately subjecting himself to the possibility of ridicule, since he must have known that as the day of the climb approached he would have a very strong temptation to back out. Knowing that most of his friends were fully aware of his intentions, he found the strength to go forward and test himself against the elements.

Make Notes to Yourself

This happens to be one of the most valuable secrets of self-discipline, and I am surprised at how few people use it. When you want to remember to do something, do not rely on your memory, particularly if it is weak.

Immediately get out a pencil and paper and make a note to yourself. You'll be amazed at how much trouble that saves you in the long run.

Einstein used to make notes to himself even when he was sailing on the lakes in Switzerland. If *he* couldn't remember all the ideas that came to him, then why should the rest of us remember all of our important ideas?

You're having dinner with your spouse and it occurs to you that you want to be sure to call the cleaners tomorrow morning to see what has happened to one of your suits. Don't rely on your memory. Get out a pad and pencil and make a note to yourself to call them in the morning. Then put the piece of paper where you know you will see it. Put it by your place at the breakfast table, with a pencil across it. When you come there next morning, it will be staring you in the face. This item, which you had completely forgotten about, will immediately be brought back to your attention, and you can take care of the matter very nicely.

Even if an idea occurs to you while you are in bed, get your body out and walk across the room if you have to and make a note to yourself. Thereafter, leave a pad and pencil by the side of the bed so you don't have to go to all the effort to wake yourself up from a nice dreamy state by walking across the room. You will often think you shouldn't go to all this trouble because you will surely remember. But take my word for it, the great majority of things like this are forgotten whether you like it or not.

I was driving from my office to attend the class that I teach, and on the way I recalled that this very subject was one I wanted to cover in this book. But I was driving and had my hands full, so I couldn't very well make notes to myself at that moment. I could have stopped, but that would have delayed me more than I thought wise just then. So I kept repeating to myself as I was driving that I wanted to get a paper and pencil and make a note to myself. After I had locked the car and was walking toward my mailbox I came across one of my students and immediately asked her for a piece of paper. She gave it to me, I made my note, and that is why I am able to write this section today, some three weeks later. I might have remembered, it is true, but in all likelihood I would have forgotten it.

Allow Yourself a Cooling-off Period

I knew a teen-ager who could not pass a clothing store window without buying something. As a result he had umpteen jackets, cowboy boots, cowboy hats, scads of pants, suits, shirts, and socks. He would charge all the things to himself but sooner or later would be unable to keep up the payments and then the bill collectors would be bothering his parents. When they learned of his indebtedness, they would practically faint. At first they would help him out or sometimes have him take the purchases back. But often enough he would find himself so tempted again that he was repeatedly buying expensive items he simply could not afford.

All of us have buying problems like this to some extent. They clearly arise from the mistaken belief that it is easier to avoid a difficult situation (such as buying to one's heart's content) than it is to face a difficult situation (such as walking past the store). If you have this problem, I have the following suggestion. Give yourself a three-day pause between the time you decide to buy an item and the time you actually commit yourself with a signature or cash.

A friend of mine took this advice quite seriously and was most grateful because of it. It seems that he and his family were looking for an automobile and they came across a very sporty, gorgeous, classy, gas-guzzling, heavy car. It did not have a great deal of luggage space, but all he could think of was how swell he would look behind the wheel of this thing going down the highway doing ninety miles an hour. The temptation to sign on the dotted line was enormous, but he was a bit afraid of how much he liked the thing and that perhaps his heart was speaking louder than his head. It was at that point that he told the salesman he would be back in three days if he was interested. By the next day he had thought over carefully how expensive the car would be, that it would require additional insurance because it was a fast sports model, that it would be a pain in the neck to take on a vacation because it did not have enough luggage space, and that within a few months he would not be as impressed by its beauty or speed as he was on first seeing it. And if that part of the appeal for the car could wear off that rapidly, then why should he subject himself to all the additional frustration that went along with it? Months later he was still glad he had used his head instead of his heart and had given himself enough time to think the matter over more carefully. The three-day pause did the trick.

I have seen this work for myself and for others in such matters as buying a house or making an investment. Unless you allow yourself time, you will find yourself being drawn by the merits of an item or a situation and failing to see some of its faults. Time is the ingredient that allows you to see the weaknesses of the item and the trouble you may be getting yourself into. Therefore, give yourself that time. You owe it to yourself. Then, if you still want to go ahead with it, at least you are aware of what you are getting.

Hero Worship

As corny as this may sound, it is still one of the important secrets for developing good self-discipline. When you have a hard task ahead and find yourself faltering, there are few things that help you as much as to realize that others whom you have admired were able to overcome the precise problem you are now facing. And if they could do it, why not you?

Earlier in this chapter I used the example of Babe Didrikson and how, despite the fact that she was a naturally endowed athlete, still had to work hard to become a champion golfer. Recall for a moment that she would go out to the golf course in the morning before going to work, be on the golf links every evening after work, and spend all her weekends hitting the ball until she blistered her hands.

It is remarkable that a woman who was so gifted in the field of athletics should have to put in that kind of effort. One could understand anyone else putting in that kind of time, but a gifted person? Yes, even a gifted person. Here she was, a born athlete, and to achieve excellence she still had to work hard, like anyone else. And it was only because she knew the value of practice and hard work that whatever gifts she had could come forth.

I have followed this example a number of times when I have found myself at a laborious and seemingly never-ending task. I simply thought of Babe Didrikson and how often she must have felt like giving up. Yet she didn't give up, and even though she had a great deal going for her without a lot of hard work, she knew that hard work was still necessary if her natural gifts were to be fully developed. So where was I getting off by doing any less? If it required that kind of dedication for her to succeed, then it would require even more for me. And if that's what it took to succeed, then I would simply have to push myself harder than I had imagined I could. I knew that if I did, I would get closer to my goal than I could possibly have imagined. And this is what has happened a number of times.

I have been trying to play Beethoven's Fifth Piano Concerto to the accompaniment of a record that has the piano part deleted. I received this as a Christmas present in December of 1972 and have played practically nothing else since that time. I am now at a point where I can manage to play most of the sections fairly decently and some even by memory. I suspect that it will take me another year or two before my playing is smooth to the point where I will feel fairly comfortable in presenting it to my small circle of friends.

The point to be borne in mind, however, is that I have experienced the most compelling kind of defeatism in trying to master this composition. I am not by any means an outstanding piano player. I have too little time and too little talent for this. Nevertheless, I have found, much to my surprise (although it shouldn't have been), that if each difficult passage was attacked one at a time and bar by bar, and if I did this often enough, I was able to play each passage at an amateurish level. This is precisely what the whole secret of self-discipline is, that *it is more important to do than to do well,* and that through practice one accomplishes mastery. However, my admiration for Babe Didrikson and her fantastic self-discipline made my task much easier. There were a number of times when I felt I had to give up and that I would never be able to master some of those difficult runs in the concerto. However, I stayed with it and worked it through. I was ready to rationalize a million times, but always I went back. To give up is momentarily a simple and easy thing to do, but I would never get anywhere that way. So I stayed with it, as Babe Didrikson stayed with her task, and am pleased to say that the way I play the piece today has no resemblance whatever to the way I played it the first few times. And on top of that, the whole experience has finally become enormously rewarding and pleasurable.

You may wonder if I've been consistent here in warning you against having to be perfect and describing what Babe Didrikson went through to be a champion. It truly appears as if she was driven by the need to excel, but in her case she had so much natural talent that she would have overridden any interference the demand for perfectionism may have created. For the rest of us, however, we can still work very hard at something without making it a necessity. Just because it is more important to do than to do well does not mean that we cannot work with dedication and purpose. As long as you are not getting all bent out of shape, not feeling desperate and depressed over your progress, you are working toward your goals in a healthy way.

5
Putting the Techniques to Work

THE HOME AND THE JOB require such repeated self-discipline that it is certainly worthwhile to give them a special section in this book. Living is simply a great deal easier if you learn to apply self-discipline in these two situations. When the following suggestions are applied you will be positively amazed at how easy it is to run both your home and your job without a great deal of strain and stress.

Pick Up as You Go

Clutter is one of the biggest headaches in a home or an office. If you put your newspaper down carelessly when you have finished reading it, you will have to come back to it sometime to pick it up. When you go to the refrigerator for catsup why not take the milk bottle with you, put it in the refrigerator, then bring the catsup back—saving yourself one trip. Then, on the way back, why not reach into the drawer where the napkins are kept and take a few with you so that you can put them around the proper places on the table? And before you sit down why don't you reach over and turn off the television? Notice how all these actions simply blend into one another and require a minimum of activity.

In some households it is possible for the housewife to do the following things when she walks from her bedroom down to the laundry room in the basement. She can pick up the dirty clothing in the laundry basket, let the dog out of the rear door as she passes through the hallway, and pick up yesterday's newspapers to be deposited on the stack of papers in the laundry room. Ordinarily persons who are not well organized would make one trip for the laundry, another to let the dog out, and a third for taking out the newspapers. All of this is wasteful, tiring and totally unnecessary.

Make it a practice to look around to see what else you could be doing at the same time you are engaged in one task or going in one direction. In fact, you will be surprised that with very little energy you can keep things neat and orderly, get things put away, and not even feel that you are working at it. How many times after a meal have you walked from the kitchen table past the sink or dishwasher? If you were to have both your hands filled with dishes each time you did that, imagine how naturally and easily the dishes would be removed and put in the dishwasher or on the kitchen counter. Since they have to be removed anyway, why not do it when you're making that move?

The same could, of course, be said for your office. Instead of making many trips from your desk to your secretary's desk, why not simply put all the items together on one corner of your desk? Then take them all at once and deposit them on her desk. If you are going down the hallway for a drink of water, take your waste-paper basket with you and empty it at the end of the hall, since it has to be done anyway. The additional energy involved is minimal, and two jobs are getting done at the same time.

The point of all this is to take advantage of any activity and get more out of it than you ordinarily would. Sure it would be easy for the moment if you didn't make the extra effort. But again it is easier to face a task than it is to avoid it.

On Tuesday You Wear the Blue Suit

Have you ever stood before a closet wondering which clothes to put on that day? Although this may happen more frequently with women, it certainly happens with men too. If you add up all the time you waste debating over which clothes to wear, which restaurant to go to, and so on, you might find yourself using up a great deal of your time in indecision.

If you are a man, there is no reason why you could not put your suits in a prearranged order. Start with Monday on the left, and so on, for as many suits as you have and then wear them in that order.

This means that when you wake up on Monday morning you go to the closet and automatically reach for the brown suit. When you take it off that night you hang it at the end of the rack to your right and push the rest of the suits over to the left. On Tuesday morning you reach for your blue suit because that is the next one. You have eliminated all that wondering what you should wear. The thinking is already done for you.

For women this may not be as easy to do because their choices are more complex. But with some imagination certain prearranged choices probably could be set up, even though from time to time, depending on the occasion and the weather, modifications might be made.

But I do have this to offer the ladies concerning breakfast. Just as we men may shift from one foot to another while we are wondering what to wear for that day, I have seen women do the same thing in front of a refrigerator at seven thirty in the morning. That indecision can be eliminated if you simply decide Monday morning to have scrambed eggs; Tuesday, kippered herring; Wednesday, cheese and toast; and so on all the way to Sunday.

In some way the same might be done for supper. There is no reason why you could not have steak on Saturday, chicken on Sunday, meatloaf on Monday, and do this for a week, ten days, or two weeks. Coming around to the same meal every ten days or two weeks is certainly not going to cause someone to hate eating. On the contrary, it might give more variety to the meals than they ordinarily would have. Leftovers do not have to throw the schedule off by being eaten the next day —they can be eaten for lunch.

Anyone who has psychological know-how may recognize in this traces of compulsive behavior, and compulsive behavior is usually thought of as neurotic behavior. Don't let that scare you. The difference between this organized behavior and neurotic compulsive behavior is that the first one makes your life easier, whereas neurotic compulsive behavior makes your life more difficult. The true compulsive can stand in front of his closet all day long and not make a decision, or if he does make it, he is always uncertain whether he should have. The healthy compulsive is the one who simply organizes himself neatly, makes this kind of chore automatic, and, by compulsively sticking to it, takes a lot of guesswork and endless decision-making from simple, everyday routines.

Recite Out Loud

One of the best ways to remember what you read or hear is literally to express the thought out loud so that you actually are listening to it. This is not quite the same as thinking the thought and then believing that you have impressed it upon your mind. There seems to be a difference between simply thinking an idea and expressing it out loud. Going through the motions of moving one's lips, exerting one's vocal cords, and actually hearing the idea expressed again over the airwaves makes the difference.

For example, I recently came across the word "pavane." I did not know what it meant, so I looked it up in the dictionary. There I discovered that it was "a stately court dance." Simply reading this definition would be the way most people would try to absorb the information. I have found, however, that by saying the definition out loud to myself or to someone else (this is even better), the tendency to remember is considerably stronger. So I then said to myself out loud, "A pavane is a stately court dance." Let me encourage you therefore to say your phone numbers or your body measurements out loud. When you are ready to buy yourself a shirt you may find that you have not forgotten the size, because you had said out loud, "My shirt size is '15½ 32.' "

You *Can* Practice Some Tasks All Day

When you want to learn a new skill, the more time you put into it the quicker you will master it. However, finding the time to practice what you are trying to learn is often a problem. There are fortunately some skills that you can practice almost all day long at sporadic times and do not require that you set aside a specific hour to practice them.

Take a language, for example. One of the best ways to learn a language is to think and speak sentences in that tongue using the foreign vocabulary over and over all day long.

If you are learning French, you could use the French word for "door" whenever you went through one. This could be done at home, at the office, even as you opened your car door. You could say the French word in an English sentence such as, "I am now opening *la porte.*" In this way you would be sure to be practicing that word, and you could practice many other words. And the practicing would go on all day long. Words that you learned which refer to dining or to table, or to utensils or food, could all be reviewed very easily while you are eating. Any words you learn that relate to dressing, clothes, fashions, could easily be rehearsed by you as you are dressing in the morning or undressing at night. And as you are driving to work or school, you could be using any word that had to do with buildings, streets, crowds, trees, houses—in short, everything that you would see in the community as you drove from the house to your place of work.

One of the Englishmen who searched for the source of the Nile River in Africa had an enormous capacity to learn languages rapidly. Apparently he could master any of the African dialects in a matter of a few months. The way he did it was to learn a few words, rehearse them repeatedly all day long, add a few more the next day, and rehearse them repeatedly. As new words were added to his vocabulary, he utilized them at every opportunity until he was reading or thinking in that language. There was enough time every day to refresh his memory for all the words and phrases he had learned that day and all those he had learned before.

Beware of Job-hopping

I have known a number of capable young men and women who simply never seemed to get ahead in life. They had reasonably good educations but were always at the bottom of the ladder vocationally, with very little prospect of getting the promotions and well-paying positions they so desperately wanted. I usually found that one of the reasons they were doing so badly was that they simply would not stay at a job they disliked until they found a better one. These people almost invariably got fed up quickly with their jobs. They convinced themselves they couldn't stand it another day, and then found themselves on the streets. They would look around for days or weeks, hungry and desperate, finally taking the first job that came along. Then this same sad set of events would occur again. They would find themselves leaving that job before they had a better one. I strongly recommend to anyone who hates his work that he had better stay with it until he finds a job that is *better* than the one he has. Rarely quit a job before you are employed somewhere else. The moment you do, you are out of work, and if not quickly reemployed, are bound to become desperate in seeking another position.

One of the brightest men I ever tested was a college graduate who was so inept with people that he did not enjoy his job in social work. He therefore resigned and tried to seek employment elsewhere. But for the next twenty-five years he never managed anything more challenging than his first job. Each successive job was more humiliating than the one before. At the time I saw him he was washing dishes part time and was spending most of the rest of his time in the public library.

During the time I counseled him, he obtained several positions but would only stay just long enough to feel insulted. He would quit and find himself on the street again. In a few weeks he'd be wishing he had kept that boring job because it was at least bringing him some money and he at least had something to do. But it made no difference in the long run. He always repeated the same regrettable hasty act and would always quit one job before he had another. I cannot recall how many times I told him never to leave one job until he had another one in the bag. But he never followed my advice. So he went on through his life griping bitterly about how the world was mistreating him, when it was obviously he who was mistreating himself.

Job-hoppers, beware! There is something wrong in your outlook if you find yourself switching all the time. It takes self-discipline to stay with a rotten job, that's true. However, if you don't do that, you will find yourself suffering a great deal more than if you had stayed with a bad job and perhaps eventually had risen through the ranks.

Achievement by Disciplined Talent

Take the case of two high school students. One is a bright fellow who never brings home a book, comes in late at night, waltzes in to class the next morning and with relatively little effort pulls down an A. The other has to study every night, denies himself the night life that his buddy has, drags himself in to class and gets a good grade but not necessarily the best.

What do you suppose often happens to persons like these when they get into college? Does the bright student still have an easy time of it and does the slower one still have to push himself like a thirsting man looking for water? No sir! What often happens is that the bright student, because he has never really developed good self-discipline, finds that when the going gets tough and his natural ability is not all *that* great, he can't sail through the work anymore. He finds himself completely bogged down and failing. He is like the hare who is so sure of winning the race that he doesn't pay much attention to it and eventually loses. The other student, the tortoise of our example, has no such illusions about his ability but at least has learned how to persevere and keep his nose to the grindstone until the job is done. When he goes to college he doesn't find the work all that different, because he learned to burn the midnight oil for several years before he entered college. Therefore he often succeeds where his brighter friend fails.

Ironically, however, the brighter student is likely to make all kinds of excuses to his friends and to himself, insisting that if he really wanted to apply himself, he certainly could. What he does not understand is that this is not true. He cannot apply himself, no matter what his talents are, unless he has first developed the self-discipline that teaches him how to apply himself. When he cavalierly says, "I could have passed that course if I had really put my mind to it," he is deceiving himself outright. If he can pass the course that easily, then why doesn't he do it? What he needs, and others need at this point, is proof of his actual ability to achieve it. If you think you could play an instrument by simply putting your mind to it, think again. Your friend knows how to play because he or she has worked endlessly at that instrument and can now perform fairly well. For you to do the same would require that you devote equal hours of practice to it.

Stop fooling yourself into thinking that all your talents are going to get you ahead. Achievement is talent plus a lot of hard work. Talent is potential that requires training, discipline, and development. I don't have to believe a thing about what you can do until you can prove to me that you can do it. Convincing me that you can do it is one thing, convincing yourself is another. Fooling me may not hurt you much, but when you fool yourself into thinking that you are only a snap of a finger away from the successful completion of a task, you are in trouble. The best and the brightest often perform the poorest because everything came too easily to them and because they believed they didn't have to prove what they could not do.

Get the Most Out of Your Studying

1. *Learn your material during the day and review it before going to sleep at night.*

Reviewing before you go to sleep what you learned during the day allows you to retain it better in the morning. Should you have an examination the next morning, the material you went over that night would be more easily recalled than if you had that examination at four o'clock in the afternoon. Having it that late in the day allows all kinds of activities to interfere with the recall of that material. Therefore, if you are going to have a test later in the day, you must be certain to review the material again shortly before taking the test.

2. *To recite or not to recite.*

Years ago a study was done with students who devoted increasing amounts of time to reciting material they had just learned. They were then tested to see how much they remembered. It was found that those who spent up to about half as much time reciting as they did studying retained the most. This means that you must allow some time to think about what you have read and to recall everything you went over. Reciting the material to yourself is actually the equivalent of giving yourself a brief quiz. It gives you feedback to see just what you have retained and what you have missed. Then you can go right back to the material and refresh your memory on any points you missed or correct any mistakes you made.

The important point is that you can spend as much as half an hour reciting material to yourself for every hour that you spend studying. If you really want to do a thorough job of understanding and remembering the material, I would advise you to do it in that way.

3. *Take a break.*

When your attention wanders from your studies, take a five- or ten-minute break as frequently as you need to. Then get back to the material refreshed and take another break as soon as your attention wanders again. I found this practice most helpful when I was doing my Ph.D. thesis in graduate school. After working on that study for some months I found myself becoming increasingly tired and even bored with it at times. The only way I could possibly finish the project was simply to take numerous breaks as my attention waned. Whenever I brought myself back to the task I was able to move on to another statistical problem or segment of the study. My attention would last a short while but then I would need to get up, stretch, have a cup of coffee, visit someone in his room for a moment, and then get back to my task. In this way the job finally got done. To have stayed with it diligently would have been sheer suffering and I'm afraid my mind simply would have wandered in any event.

4. *Massed vs. spaced practice*

Whenever you have to learn something that requires repetition, such as poetry, dates, or chemical formulas, you always have the choice of practicing for long stretches at a time or practicing for brief but frequent periods. If, for example, you have to write a paper, first write out a broad outline. Later you can leisurely spend a little time on the various subheadings. The same is true about practicing a piece of music. Spaced (or distributed) practice is helpful in this case because music can be broken up into melodies and phrases or simply into pages. Ultimately you can bring all these separate parts together by massed practice so that you develop a unity and a harmony uniting all the parts.

Spaced practice is especially good with tasks that do not make a great deal of sense. For example, if you had to remember many numbers or chemical formulas, distributed practice would be a great deal better than massed practice. You could say these numbers to yourself at any free moment during the day. Expecting to remember dozens of telephone numbers, for example, or dozens of chemical formulas at one sitting, simply is highly inefficient. But to do this over a period of hours, days, or even weeks is much easier.

Easy material should be learned in one sitting, whereas difficult material is best practiced a little at a time. Problem-solving is also best handled if it is done at one time unless, of course, you simply get stuck in a rut. At that point it may be practical to take a break and come back to the problem refreshed. In the time that you are gone you may be surprised at the insights that develop and the new approaches you can bring to your problem.

5. *Don't depend upon cramming the night before.*

Practically all students cram for their examinations the night or the morning before. Nothing I can say is going to change this a great deal, because we all have a tendency to procrastinate anyway. Moreover, there seems to be good reason to believe that some cramming is helpful and efficient. However, woe to the student who depends solely upon cramming to learn his material. He will find that unless he has spent a good deal of time trying to learn the information long before the eve of the exam, he is going to be in a bad way. Cramming has the following disadvantages: it tends to be inefficient, the learning is usually under stress and is therefore less enjoyable, and it emphasizes memory rather than understanding.

Therefore, if you want to do the best you can before a test, make sure you have reviewed the material with distributed practice days or weeks before. Then spend some time the night before the exam bringing the level of retention up to an acceptable level. But usually this does not require intense boning up until three o'clock in the morning. It is simply a matter of refreshing the mind with facts that are lying there like wilted flowers that only need a spurt of water to revive them to a lively, healthy condition.

6. *Stick to one task at a time.*

All students are soon caught in the dilemma between doing one thing and then finding that they have to drop that to do another. Soon they are entangled in several activities at once and then find that they are busy all the time but not getting anything done. How does one handle these conflicting motives?

In my experience I have found that it is best for a person not to take on too many things at one time. Instead, make sure that what you start you try to finish. In the writing of this book, for example, I have often been tempted to put the task aside. But had I done so, I would ultimately have delayed the finishing of the book by many months and this I found undesirable. Therefore, since I had this unfinished business at hand I went on working so that I could get it out of the way. When the book is finished I will then turn to other things in which I am interested.

This still allows me to intersperse other activities into this business of writing a book. Since I generally use distributive practice, there is always some time between my efforts when I could take up other issues if they do not become all-absorbing. For example, in between those days when I am not dictating or writing on this book I am perfectly free to write articles and to carry out my practice in general. But when the pages come back from my secretary they need proofreading. Then I must set aside those other things to some extent so that I can again work on this task. If I do not give it proper priority, it simply does not get done and all kinds of other activities take precedence. Anytime something serious comes up I can always put it aside and pick it up when the crisis is over. And I can do this all the more comfortably because I know I have been diligent on my project when I have had the time to devote to it.

Therefore, be careful that you do not have too many irons in the fire. You cannot do everything or be everything you would like to be. There are only so many hours in a day and so many days in your life. When you start something, try to finish it and then go on to something else that absorbs you. Occasionally allow critical matters to intrude into that plan, but, in the main, have tunnel vision. Have single-mindedness of purpose. Always think of finishing the project. Imagine how it will be when you are done, what the benefits will be, how wonderful you will feel when it is finished, and how you can then look forward to doing something else pleasurable. Do not let yourself get drawn toward another pleasurable activity until you have finished the first or else you will always be bouncing from one pleasurable activity to another and seldom finishing a single thing. All activities have moments of boredom or difficulty. If you let those temporary moments of displeasure color your whole outlook, you will always give up what you are doing in favor of something else which seems for the moment more attractive. You will find that you will have no sense of accomplishment, because you have become what all self-disciplined people shun most of all and that is to become a dilettante.

7. *Small amounts of tension assist learning.*

Some persons feel that they can learn best when everything is absolutely quiet. However, when they are sitting in their favorite armchair with their book in hand, and believe that now they can be totally absorbed in their studies, they are likely to fall asleep. The best studying is done under slight tension. This is why having the radio on softly not only drowns outside noises but forces the person to overcome the distraction from the radio itself so that he concentrates all the more vigorously on the material at hand.

8. *Reward yourself after you have performed.*

I recently learned about a man who took his family out for dinner because it looked as though he might land a very nice job. Understand now, he didn't have the job, there was only a good possibility that he might get it. He was rewarding himself for something that had not yet happened.

I find this unwise because it causes people to be lax. If you are rewarded before you have earned it, you let down your drive and do not do all you otherwise might. In other words do not reward yourself with a movie until you have done all your studying for the night. Do not go out with the boys for a relaxing time until you have completed all your assignments. If you want to put off studying until tomorrow morning and go out with the boys tonight, you may have to pay the price. There will be less time in the morning to study, it will be more hectic you may have to nurse a hangover. Worst of all, you have allowed yourself to have a good time without fully earning the right to do so. You are in school not to have fun but to get an education. Only when you have satisfied the requirements that can lead to this goal do you have the moral right to please yourself with nights out on the town.

9. *Reward yourself mentally.*

One of the neatest things about our brain is the fact that we can punish or reward ourselves with our own thoughts. All of us are pretty good about punishing ourselves and this is one of the most common human activities. What you can practice more, however, is rewarding yourself when you have done well. You can do that by thinking pleasant thoughts, calling yourself nice names, imagining people appreciating you, getting all kinds of attention and fame, or even just thinking of beautiful things such as scenery, food, or art.

For example, when you have done your night's studying, reward yourself mentally by imagining yourself going up for your degree on commencement day. Or imagine yourself being called up in front of the class for earning the highest grades. Or reward yourself with the thought of becoming an expert in something and being called in by the government to provide expert testimony at fantastic fees. Daydream if you like. A daydream is like a reward. It shapes our goals for us at the deepest levels. And who does not enjoy a daydream? Pat yourself on the back, therefore, when you have done something well, because others often do not, even though they may admire you for what you have achieved. The world is quick enough to condemn for what you do wrong, so be quick to reward yourself for what you do right.

If rewarding yourself mentally isn't all that satisfying, then by all means reward yourself materially. Buy yourself something, take a vacation, have a date, but do something good for yourself. It is perfectly legitimate and it makes a stronger person of you. Do not feel guilty for wanting to be good to yourself.

6
A Student Struggles with Self-Discipline

THIS IS THE CASE of Mr. B., with whom I have had several sessions. He has just mentioned his first week in college. The client's problem so far has been his inability to apply himself to subjects he does not like. In the following remarks the reader is advised to observe how Mr. B. (*a*) talks himself into poor self-discipline and (*b*) how I try to get him to question his self-defeating philosophies. These are: he must like an activity if he is to do well at it; getting even with others is more important than treating himself well; and avoiding the task of temporary suffering or discomfort is better than facing a tough task.

This session will not demonstrate any great strides over his problem. Rather, it points out how doggedly he and the therapist must go over the same ground time and again until after many more weeks the improvement becomes noticeable and lasting.

THERAPIST: How have you been doing?
CLIENT: Okay.
T: You mentioned that you liked school so far and I

111

suggested that that was not terribly important. Right?

C: Right. But to me, liking something *is* important, because when I was in junior high school I didn't like some classes and flunked them. But in the classes I liked, I got A's. The counselors didn't know what was going on inside my head. They had a lot of meetings with my mom and me. They couldn't figure it out and I just told them I didn't like the classes, so I didn't do any work.

T: So you're potentially heading for a big fall at college if you do the same thing there. Isn't that true?

C: Yes, that's true. But I've matured a little bit since I was in junior high, I think, and I might be able to handle those classes I don't like.

T: How?

C: By just doing the work.

T: Yes, but you still have the habit of *not* doing things you dislike. How are you going to switch from leaving things alone that you don't like to literally doing them carefully, spending a lot of time on them, and working hard at things you hate? How are you going to switch from one to the other?

C: By disciplining myself to do it. Don't put it off.

T: What's going to make you do that now? You knew that much in high school, didn't you?

C: Yes.

T: It didn't help you in high school, why should it help you in college.

C: High school is important, but college is important too. There is the grade aspect of it. Future employers are going to look at the grades that I got. If they see a bad grade in one subject and a good grade in another, and if they need both of these subjects for me to do a job, they are not going to want me, because I am not good in both.

112

T: Well, possibly, but more serious than that is the need to get passing grades or you won't even get the degree at all. You want to pass. What sort of thing did you do well in high school? You say you flunked three courses.

C: German II, Algebra, and English.

T: And you didn't like them?

C: I didn't like the teacher. I really hated her.

T: Now, is it important to like the teacher?

C: It used to be. It's not really that way anymore.

T: You now think that even if you don't like the teacher you can still make good grades in a subject?

C: Yes.

T: What did you tell yourself before that made you get poor grades to spite the teacher? How did you use that as a reason?

C: I just didn't like her.

T: Therefore . . .

C: Well, I just sat there in class. I did the work in class but I wouldn't do any homework. She used to get mad because I didn't do any homework. It didn't bother me at all though, really.

T: Why not?

C: I wasn't thinking about the future, so it didn't bother me.

T: Are you thinking about the future now?

C: Yes.

T: If that's true, then I'd say you probably won't goof off. That's the whole trick in terms of being disciplined, whether or not you have your eye on the future, whether you are going to take your pleasures sometime in the future or whether you insist upon having them right now. But there is another part to your problem. You think that you *have* to like whatever you are doing.

That is a very bad and erroneous conclusion. Michelangelo didn't like painting the Sistine Chapel, for example. Do you know what I am talking about?

C: Yes.

T: He didn't like that. He wanted to quit. In fact, he didn't like it but he created a masterpiece. So go ahead and dislike your classes. What's that got to do with learning and applying yourself? And if you do that, incidentally, what is going to happen?

C: I will be able to handle other situations much better.

T: Yes, but you might also get to like them. You don't like algebra, for example. What happens, typically, when you don't like algebra? Do you do much of it?

C: No.

T: Right. You don't do the work at home, you don't crack the books, you don't ask questions about it, you don't stop and think about what the whole business behind algebra is. Not doing that, you go to class the next day less prepared than you were the day before. There is no moving ahead, and you know less and less about it. Correct? So you tend to hate it more, don't you? Okay. But hating it more during the class that day, do you do more or less of it that night because you hate it?

C: Less.

T: You do less of it. Doing less of it, you become more hostile toward it and you do still less of it. You can't help winding up doing less and less in something while disliking it more and more. That's the cycle. Now suppose you took it the other way around. Suppose you said, "Okay, I hate it. However, I am going to work harder. I still want to get an A." So you do more of it. Doing more and working harder at it can help you to know it a little better. And when you go back to class the next day you can volunteer, you can be interested. And being interested, you get to what?

C: You get to like it.

T: You get to like it a little bit. Getting to like it a little bit, you tend to go home that night and maybe put more time in on the homework. You come back to class in the morning and you can understand the work a little bit better. It makes sense. You can begin to take a little pride in your work. You answer a few more questions. You begin to what? Like it again a little more. What usually happens as you work at something is that you get better at it. When you get better at something, you tend to like it more. So your dislike seems to be revolving around two things: the subject matter (which you start out disliking) and, secondly, you used the subject as the means of hurting the teacher. "I'll show her! I don't like her. I'm not going to cooperate with someone I don't like."

C: It was a man for algebra.

T: Oh. But the German teacher was female?

C: Yes. As well as the English teacher. I just did not learn German.

T: Yes, but why not? You didn't work at it.

C: Yes. Right.

T: You didn't work at it because you didn't like it. You're using the idea that if you don't like something, you shouldn't have to work at it. How can you possibly get to like something until you work at it whether you like it or not? It's like saying it's going to be cold this winter. So what else is new? See? Of course you're going to dislike some courses. That doesn't mean anything. What are you going to school for anyway, to like subjects?

C: Yes.

T: Are you really?

C: I'm not working for a degree right now.

T: Well, what are you going for?

C: I'm just taking some subjects to learn things I want to learn.

T: Oh. You are not going for a degree at all?

C: No.

T: Okay. Your problem is different then. Then you are simply going for the pleasure of it. Right?

C: Yes. You could say that.

T: Well, what for? Why are you going for the pleasure of it?

C: Just to learn some things I don't know and want to learn.

T: Like what?

C: I'm taking a math course. It's pretty technical mathematics. You get into some algebra and trigonometry.

T: Why would you want that?

C: To learn some math. I've got all kinds of math books at home because I might take a radio and television engineering course and if I do, then I need math as a prerequisite.

T: Yes, but you are talking about eventually needing this stuff to make a living.

C: Yes.

T: So it is still something that is not just for the pure pleasure of it. You are taking this for an ulterior motive.

C: I am taking all of these courses for an ulterior purpose.

T: Yes. For a career. Now we are back to where we started. It doesn't matter whether you like the teacher. You're going there to learn, aren't you? Do you have to like what you are learning?

C: No.

T: No. It's got relatively little to do with it. It makes it better and easier if you like the subjects and the teachers. It's like saying, "It would be nice if I had to take medicine that tasted good." But suppose it doesn't taste good. Does that change the fact that you had better take it?

C: No.

T: Not really, does it? For example, you play the guitar, right? I don't suppose you've always enjoyed playing it. Surely you sometimes had to practice even when you were not in the mood for it?

C: Yes.

T: Then you must have said something like: "I'd really like to learn how to play the guitar and if I keep working at it, even during periods when I don't particularly like to, then I will eventually become a good guitar player and that will give me a great deal of enjoyment later in my life. Right now I don't really feel like playing a guitar but I can't always use this excuse, 'I don't feel like it.'" You just went ahead and did it anyhow, didn't you? You must have done that. If you practiced only when you felt like it, how much time would you have put in?

C: I do it a lot because I like it a lot.

T: Guitar playing?

C: Yes.

T: Okay, probably with guitar playing you do. But even so, I am sure that every time you picked up your guitar you haven't enjoyed it. You had to put some time in to keep your fingers tough and to learn the technique. So it took a lot of work, and not all of it was pleasant. You simply disciplined yourself and you said sensibly, "Well, I have to do this if I want the reward

117

later." It *is* easier to do it this way, you see. That is the whole point. It is literally *easier* for you to knock yourself out now and think of the long-range goals rather than the short-range goals. It's the same thing we talked about with your smoking. How are you doing on that?

C: Terrible.

T: Go ahead.

C: It's still the same. Smoking the same—a pack a day. Also I have a cold. I just have a little cough left now, which doesn't help matters any. I smoke, and it irritates me more and more. I just keep doing it though.

T: Let's not get into that right now. How are you going to make the most out of your experiences in college? What is very important for you to do? What is the key here we've been talking about?

C: Work.

T: To do the work. To discipline yourself and not just slough off because you happen not to like a teacher. Nobody said college is supposed to be nice. Nobody said it is supposed to be fun. Nobody said it is even supposed to be interesting. I guess it depends upon you. There it is—just a subject. Whether the subject is interesting or not depends on what you invest in it, doesn't it?

C: That's right.

T: And if it isn't interesting to you, what must you do?

C: Work at it. Try to make it interesting.

T: How does a person develop interest in a subject?

C: Work hard at it.

T: You have to work harder at that very thing which is so boring. I know you wouldn't do this, but notice how silly it sounds if put in another context. If your right arm were stronger than your left, which arm would you use more often?

C: The right, of course.

118

T: Now suppose you wanted to strengthen the left arm.

C: I'd have to use it practically all the time and exercise it. Work at it and make it stronger.

T: You have to keep lifting with the one that is weak. It's no different in school. You have to work at things that you don't like. That's the way you get to master them.

C: Right.

T: Now, can you see what philosophical notion you want to fight in order to discipline yourself? What is that one neurotic thought which all people convince themselves is true?

C: Is it about fear, that if there is something you fear, you should always—

T: No, you're talking about fear. That if something awful might happen, you should worry about it. That will only lead to fear. I'm asking what leads to poor self-discipline, the sort of thing you are continually fighting. Do you recall it? No? Let me spell it out carefully for you. Listen to this: *It is the idea that it is easier to avoid a difficult situation than it is to face it.* You have your boring, difficult algebra in front of you. But you could be playing your guitar. Now the question is, which is the easier thing to do, drop the algebra book and pick up the guitar, or study the algebra and leave the guitar alone until later? Which is really easier? Well, the neurotic idea says it is easier to avoid a difficult situation than it is to face it. Therefore you drop the algebra book and pick up the guitar and have a good time. Correct? But I say that is neurotic. That is poor self-discipline. That is damaging to you.

C: Yes.

T: The easier thing is to literally what?

C: Study harder so you know more about it.

T: Studying harder so you will enjoy it more and then you will be relaxed and you can always play your guitar anyway, can't you?

C: Yes.

T: Go study harder. Face the difficult situation. That is the easier thing to do. You *face* the problem, not run away from it. Now do you get it?

C: Yes.

T: The same thing is true with your smoking. When you reach for a cigarette you are again doing the hard thing, not the easy or healthy thing. Right now it is pleasant, but in the long run it is going to be damaging. It just depends on when you want the payoff. If you want the payoff right now, you will pay dearly later. If you want the payoff later on, fine, it doesn't cost you as much. This is the basis of the discipline problem: whether you want to avoid a difficult problem and feel that it is easier to avoid it rather than face it. I say face it. Don't run away from it. Do the hard thing, because in the long run it is usually the easiest action. Take the long easy way out rather than the short hard way. Okay? I don't want to run that theme into the ground. Maybe you want to talk about something else now?

7
Final Remarks

There Is No Other Way

The tendency to believe in magic to help us with our problems is so strong that nothing but the most painful experiences sink through to the point where we finally give up believing in Alice in Wonderland. Many find it difficult to realize that it is a pretty hard world out there. Unless you accept it as that, it's going to run right over you. By this I mean that overreliance on people is not the answer. Taking endless tranquilizers is not the answer. Drinking yourself half to death over your problems is not the answer. Running away from one job to another whenever the job is unpleasant is not the answer. Last, but not least, allowing yourself to have a nervous breakdown to rationalize your failures or to escape an unpleasant situation is not the answer either.

This last maneuver, our profession has increasingly come to realize, is one that people use to solve their problems. One of my clients was the community champion at having emotional breakdowns whenever things became tense. I repeatedly accused him of using his emotions as a way of escaping from the unpleasantries of life, such as having to get a job, standing up to his wife, cleaning the garage, and so on. But he managed to get around every one of them, saying that he wasn't feeling well and therefore couldn't get a job, he was too weak to paint the house, or he was too upset to do the things expected of a normal adult. As long as he had the old mental illness bugaboo to throw around, he could get away with murder.

After I had tried on numerous occasions to get him to see that he was using his emotional disturbances as a means of manipulating his world, he finally caught on. He brought in a large piece of felt on which he had painted a thought which he had read recently. It went something like this: "When these pressures are gone, when things settle down a bit, I am going to have myself a nervous breakdown. I've worked hard for it, I am entitled to it, and no one's going to take it away from me."

In your task to discipline yourself, be sure you are not defeating your very best efforts by failing to recognize your need to have emotional problems because they can come in handy at times. Obviously what is necessary to help you at that point is for you to learn to get over your neurotic hang-up before you attempt anything else.

Betty was one of those persons who went around endlessly complaining about how miserable her life was and how good it would be if only things could be different. I tried to show her over and over that she had as many breaks as anybody else but that because she was so filled with fear, because she was terrified of rejection, and because she would feel guilty if she didn't do everything perfectly, she walked off jobs before they were mastered. She would not apply for jobs because she was sure she would not be hired. So she went on complaining bitterly about how rotten her life was, how bored she was with the jobs she occasionally managed to get, and why did the world treat her so badly? She would not believe me when I told her that she would have to change her neurotic thinking whether she liked it or not. That was the only way she was ever going to make the greatest use of her considerable potential. She had attended college but had to drop out for the reasons she dropped everything else: fear and poor self-discipline.

One of the last times I saw her she was in one of my groups complaining as she usually did of having been unemployed for a year. I heard her say that she wanted to work as a clerk-typist. Knowing of such an opening, I had her leave the group room at that very moment to call the office I mentioned. She returned, saying that the office would be glad to interview her in a couple of hours. I suggested she keep that appointment as soon as group therapy was over. It turned out that she did indeed get the job. However, she was on the job for three hours when she ran across a task with which she was unfamiliar, and felt so uncomfortable with it she became upset. She instantly rationalized that she couldn't possibly work as an upset person and therefore would have to leave. So three hours after she landed a gem of a job, she quit.

There is no other way for her to become a mature and strong person except to finally recognize that she is a first-class neurotic. Nothing but very hard work, facing her fears, and discipling herself severely is ever going to change things. Landing jobs isn't going to do it. Coming to psychotherapy by itself is not going to do it. Crying endlessly to herself is not going to do it. Medicine may not do it. Becoming a mature and self-disciplined person requires work, a lot of it. Often that work is done under trying conditions, and during periods when we are all very upset. Tough. That's the way it is, and the sooner we recognize that life can be pretty tough on us and that growth can still take place even though we are mightily disturbed, the sooner we will outgrow these neurotic tendencies. Never think that this is heaven when it is only imperfect earth with all its injustices and all its neurotic people to make it pretty much of a madhouse at times. The only way you will make it better is to stop fanciful wishing and see the world exactly as it is. Nothing short of facing your problems and changing your neurotic ideas into rational ones is going to do the job.

Afterthoughts

To overcome a crushing depression or guilt, to overcome hostility and the bitterness that comes of being treated unjustly, requires nothing less than great self-discipline. No matter how much you want to conquer your disturbances, you will continue to suffer with all of them unless you learn to apply these principles.

Does this mean that you should never get upset, that you should never even feel nervous, that you are not disciplining yourself if you do have those feelings? I raise this question because of what a number of people who have read my other books have said. To them I leave the impression that once we understand how we get upset, we must never again even feel anything like a disturbance coming on or else we are obviously not practicing what I am preaching, we are not disciplining ourselves.

That is not the case. If I have given this impression, I apologize, and I want to correct this immediately. Remember always that you cannot correct an emotional disturbance *until you first feel that you have one.* How can you work on feelings of depression unless you first notice that you are getting depressed? How can you squelch your anger unless you realize that you are already allowing yourself to become somewhat angry? Once you notice these moods developing, get on top of the problem quickly before it gets out of hand and starts to hurt you. The beginning of a depressive feeling is hardly serious, but if you don't catch it in the bud and talk yourself out of it, if you fail to apply yourself with diligence and discipline, you are going to allow that little bit of depression to grow much bigger.

It is therefore safe to say that many of us who practice rational-emotive therapy are frequently tense, angry, or depressed. But we are better trained to work on these *beginning* emotions quickly and to annihilate them than is the ordinary citizen. Having neurotic feelings to a minor degree is inescapable. So the next time you notice that you are getting upset, don't let that mere observation throw you. Simply recognize that a neurotic reaction is emerging but that you now can have the knowledge to combat practically all the ordinary types of emotional reactions that you are likely to encounter in almost any day of your life. Then, with the self-discipline that you have been reading about in this book, you can apply what you learned until you actually remove the small amount of neuroticism you were beginning to feel. When you have done that, it is safe to say that you are certainly on your best way to becoming a very strong and emotionally stable human being.

A Word of Caution

Now that I have gone to some effort to tell you about how to discipline yourself, I want to end the book by cautioning you not to overdo a good thing. Overdiscipline is sometimes as bad or even worse than no discipline. Just as poor self-discipline can rob you of happiness, so can overdiscipline spoil your enjoyment of life. Take the case of Bob. Everything he did, he did with an intensity that was unbelievable. When he took up bowling it wasn't enough that he immediately bought a bowling outfit, a ball and new shoes, but he joined not one bowling league but five. When he went to a movie that he enjoyed, he saw it two or three times in one night. At the time that he was setting up his own business, he stayed at it day and night for the first month until it got solidly on its feet. There was apparently no moderation in this man. He did not know how to gauge a thing sensibly so that he could engage in an activity and enjoy life at the same time. Everything had a desperate quality about it that exhausted him in whatever he attempted.

Why are some people like this? Bob was a fellow who had always been lazy as an adolescent but was still sharp enough to realize what all his goofing off had done to him. Determined never to harm himself like that again, he set a course of self-discipline for himself that was monkish in style. He became so overdisciplined that he was no fun to be with, his family could not break into his routine, and he became a physical and emotional wreck in the process.

There is a well-known saying, "All things in moderation." Just because you are interested in a program of self-improvement does not mean that you have to go so far overboard that you make yourself chronically miserable. If you want to be a more productive person, be careful that you discipline yourself within *reasonable* limits. Despite what I said previously about slips adding up, it is still important to take occasional vacations and goof off briefly from rigorous routines. But always beware of the danger of backsliding. Then, if you can bring yourself back on target, do not hesitate to paint a ceiling, climb a mountain, or break a world record. Good luck on your quest to find out all that you are capable of and in making yourself do what you want to do.